The Gift

Travis McLaurin

Print information available on the last page.

Rev. date: 07/19/2022

To order additional copies of this book, contact:
Xlibris
844-714-8691
www.Xlibris.com
Orders@Xlibris.com
827367

The book is dedicated to Geraldine C McLaurin…
She's only sleeping…

CONTENTS

"I am the Gift. I am just what he's been waiting for".
Not gold. Or Shining jewels. I am the Gift that he's been
longing for. I brought my Gift to give to him. But all he did was
touch my hand. Can't you see? All I need to bring is me."

Travis Mclaurin - The Great Late Potentate. St. Ann School Children's Christmas Musical-December 1983.

I guess that was a prophecy. A prophecy that I sung those lyrics that Monday night years ago as a child of 13. I've always believed that. Throughout the 50 years of my life, I struggled with myself as far accepting who I am. There are certain people on this earth who are "The Gift". When I performed that musical, I was taken off the Basketball Team when I was member just for only 2-3 weeks. The reason was forging my father's name on a progress report of Science Class because my grade average was 73 = D. It really tore me apart. Sister Saundra, a nun, the principal of my school, St Ann Catholic School has told me that I would no longer be on the team. Science was a very difficult subject for me in the 7th grade. I, being mischievous and my unruly, Manic Behavior that my teachers was trying to figure me out during my attendance there, (August 1976-June 1985). But that was to be put to rest when I admitted to the Forsythe-Stokes Mental Health on Monday, February 19, 1996 in Winston-Salem, NC.

I guess it's important to begin my journey to tell you about myself from the time I was born to that early sunny cool spring-like day of February.

You have to start somewhere. There's always a Beginning.

FAYETTEVILLE, NC 1970 - WINSTON-SALEM, NC 1996

As this third child born of the late Geraldine Cameron McLaurin, 29, my mother, of Godwin, NC on Tuesday, June 16, 1970. 10:43am at the Cape Fear Valley Hospital (Now Cape Fear Medical Center), Fayetteville, NC, My Father, William H. McLaurin, 31, of Eastover, NC just started working at a new job, Kelly-Springfield Tire Company (now Good Year) was a true Blessing for him. Being employed there for just nearly 3 months, I was his "good luck charm". A new child just born and a new good paying job. He was blessed. A dedicated Man who put all his hard earned time and work, to the Plant that manufacture Tires for cars. Six years later my mother would be employed there in late summer of August 1976.

I am the youngest of 3 children. My 2 oldest sisters, Gail "Teasie" Yolanda and Tonya. Eleven-year old Teasie was very excited to learn that she has a "Baby Brother" and Tonya who just turned three, I guess she didn't know what was going on. She later told me she knew I was born but she couldn't figure it out what was going on. My parents named me, William Travis McLaurin. Though, unfortunately, my Family had no knowledge that this infant boy was born with a chemical imbalance in his brain.

Now, Life on this earth was in the midst of change. Especially, in the US. I'm one of the Generation X, a term for Baby Boomers who was born during the height of the Civil Rights Era. The late 1960's to the 1970's. Racial Violence was prevalent which is still a problem today. The Assassinations of our two best leaders divided and saddened us. Riots erupted in major cities. Unrest was still dragging in a little country in Southeast Asia. Sending poor boys over to that country to fight, serve and perish as our young America at home was opposed and trying to figure out why we were there. As they returned home, they were unwanted and mentally broken. Integration of public schools, neighborhoods was more noticeable. A historical Music Festival was taken place in Upstate Bethel, New York, proving to the world that all people, a generation of black and white could live together in "Peace and Harmony". LOVE, SEX and PEACE. A radical African-American political organization was shouting and protesting "POWER TO THE PEOPLE!!" for the injustices in America. A highly influential and beloved Rock Band from Liverpool, England decided to call it day and "Let It Be". We successfully put a Man on the Moon, as the astronaut uttered, "That's one small step for man, one giant leap for mankind." A left-handed black guitarist from Seattle, Washington who played a crazy Fender Stratocaster of heavy blues and psychedelic rock and kissed the sky. A soul-blues woman from Port Arthur, Texas proudly sung "Piece of my heart". Her whole heart was taken. A former film student from Melbourne, Florida turned leader and singer of a rock band. The Doors. His wild personality and outrageous presence on stage captivated the rock music scene. Three of them died young at the age of 27. Tinsletown was entering the new decade. The '70's. With unforgettable and highly acclaimed films in the history of cinema. A children's Television Show inspired Kids like me watching and singing, "Sunny Day Sweepin the Clouds away. On my way to where the air is sweet. Could you tell me how to get? How to get to Sesame Street?" Just as A kind gentle young man would come to his home with a Bright smile, just simply asking, "Please won't you be? My neighbor." Saturday Morning Cartoons aired on CBS, ABC and NBC was definitely mandatory. Soul/R&B Music was Swinging and being highly appreciated by White Americans. A "Hippest Trip in America" Television show was presented every Saturday Afternoon of African-American Teens dancing and developing styles with their Bell bottoms and Afros. Five Young Brothers from Gary, IND, was exploding everywhere in the music scene. Folk Music was trying to point out the essence of life. A paranoid President of the US was caught interfering the election of 1972. With all his men being brought to justice. He resigned from office in disgrace. A new style of music, dance craze was forming in clubs during the middle of the 70's called "DISCO".

That what was prevailing during my life as my Parent's was raising and taking care of me.

Now getting back to THE GIFT, as I was growing up as a child I really didn't seem view myself as a GIFT. I was just living an innocent life as regular children did. But all through my life attending Parochial School I always knew that I was "Different". Being "Different" to most of the people that I've met, did not accept me. It was primarily out of rejection and cruelty. Thinking very deeply about that would ensure me that everyone is treated a certain way and it always depend on how you carry yourself. What you have, what you do in life and Impartially to that Being Judged. In my traumatic past, I came across people who deeply inspired me. Especially, at my grade school, the children were good and bad. As I grew to an adult, they did the same. They reached out and touched me. I was raised in a Roman Catholic Family. My parents when they moved to Fayetteville, NC. They went to a small church that catered African-Americans. As they grew up in a segregated atmospheric South, got married and had a family of their own. They did what they had to do as they were raised by their parents to be good. Yes, Yes. Be Good. Being Good. Is that a Problem to others? At that little church and the school on 357 N. Cool Spring Street that had values that was instilled in me. I never consider myself fortunate. I knew what was good and bad. I lived and learned but it took time. My father would always tell me, "You're just as good as anybody". My parents raised me to the best to their tendency.

I am Somebody. I am a Human Being that wants to live a modest normal life. Not perfect but be happy.

During my Childhood, where I lived was at 734 Eufaula Street in Fayetteville, NC. My neighborhood was called, "THE BOTTOM".

Yes, it was the "Hood". A place out of nowhere. It was located near downtown Fayetteville and my school, St. Ann Catholic School. "The Bottom" had some characters, of course being populated with African-Americans. Right up from my home was a public school Called TC. Berrien Elementary School. My sister Tonya attended there not me. Around my little neighborhood, the neighbors were bad and a few was good. Everything was just going along. Something was always happening. A regular different neighborhood that my parents sheltered me from most of the people.

With our little house, decorated perwinkle blue. The front door was red and a rocking chair stood in front side of the door. To the right was a big Magnolia tree that I always climbed on. The bees would get their nutrients from the white flowers during the spring. Also, in the front of our house was two bushes of Azaleas that would also bloom Light pink in the spring. The left side was a patio where our cars parked and a telephone pole stood next to the road with the fence along with it. Over the years, My parents added rooms to the house because Tonya and I were growing up as kids. Teasie barely out of her teens and she would attend Methodist College (Methodist University) and then join the US Navy.

I, Your Friendly Narrator sharing with you, his "Different" life was just living his life. As a child, I developed my strong resemblance to my late fragile mother, "GERALDINE" as I was always called by her side of the Family, all my life. My mother's side of the Family had strong "DNA". My Maternal Grandparents were Lonnie Cameron (1896-1968) and Daisy Smith (1903-1990) bore 15 children (one child died in infancy). My mother was the eleventh child of 14 children. My grandparents bore ten daughters and four sons. Four are alive and still kicking. With a large Brood of Grandchildren everywhere. To be honest with you, I have first cousins that I don't know to this day. They knew me when I was a child but I don't remember them. But I always welcomed them. I can only say this about my mother's side they are very open-minded. Now, my Dad's side was different. He was the eighth Child of 11 by his parents, (two died in infancy) and he had two "outside siblings". A half sister and a half brother. He was called "HODGES" by his Family. My paternal Grandparents were, James (PK) McLaurin (1897-1973) and Almeta Jane Spearman, (1900-1983), My Father was raised in Eastover, NC, not too far from my mother. I can express about my Father's side was they were loyal, trustful and definitely believed in Family. Respect was important on both sides. Both my Grandfathers were Farmers. My maternal grandmother, "Grand Ma Daisy" lived at the little shack near the Elizabeth AME Zion Church, in Godwin, NC, which is part of my Grandparents land. Lonnie Cameron was a WWI veteran and he was highly respected. From what I heard about him was that He was a "quiet man" an introvert, soft spoken. A good man and he would do anything good for you. Also, from what my sister Teasie and Aunt Lueretta, told me that he stayed in the house while his large brood of children worked out in the field. He died before I was even born. I strongly believed he suffered from Post Traumatic Stress Disorder because back then, Being a black child with strict parents who believed in discipline, respect, you never talked back or questioned your parents. Definitely, the same with my Father's Family. Mental disorders was inherited from my mother's side. Back then in the Jim Crow law Era, African-Americans had no choice but to bond together. Majority of them Migrated from the Racist South to the North and to the West for a Better life and better opportunities but to continue experience racial discrimination. My Dad's Family was more talkative and clownish, but very loyal. They attended Shiloh Church of Christ in Vander, NC. My grandfather "PK" was a true man. Strongly believed in respect and discipline as well. He was good people. All through my life I heard nothing but good things about him. He was a "Rolling Stone".

As for me? The person that I am today, I must admit I inherited all those attributes from them. I can go back as 3-4 years old. I do remember running around alot in our little house. Teasie told me that I was a "Happy Baby". That I would bump and injure my head alot from time to time. Probably, one of the main causes because I think from my first therapist "Pam' told me when a child is born, it is still developing. The head of a child is under the process in development.

My father later said it took time to "potty train" me. Also, I went
through periods of Vertigo, sensations swirling around me. My sisters
would put a wig on my head from time to time and they tease me
jokingly about my strong resemblance to my mother. And I wasn't
concentrating or focused. My pediatrician, Dr. Shaw would examine
me and my behavior was extreme "Hyperactive' (you're going to hear
alot of this word). He was the leading pediatricians in Fayetteville.
Tonya later told me that he couldn't conclude my problem much
at least give a diagnosis of me. I got spanked alot by my hard stern
Father during this time and I guess that early stages of my growth.
It deeply effected me. Now, I would get really mad at him for doing
that. Now you must understand, African-American Fathers during
that time had responsibilities disciplining their children. I was a
highly fragile and sensitive child it left deep scars on me to this day.
Teasie also told me I was still drinking out of a bottle until I was
2-3 years old when my Grandmother Daisy took it away from me.
My mother didn't approve of that. Now, My mother was fragile and
very very sensitive, she was overly protective of me. All her siblings
knew that Geraldine Cameron McLaurin looked after this 3rd child
of hers. "Her Baby". There was no doubt I belonged to her. That's
main reason I am called to this day, "GERALDINE". I would go to
extreme rages as a child when I was angry. So, as a child, from that
early on it was like that people couldn't figure me out I would assume.
Being mischievous and in a world of confusion, as to no clue of about
my whereabouts I suffered.

I never attended kindergarten, only my sisters did. As my parents
were working tirelessly to raise their Family of three, We had to deal
with those "characters' in our neighborhood. I remember. Those
characters would harass us when we weren't doing anything to
nobody during the 70's. We kept to ourselves. We were private. But
good people. I do remember vaguely my parents would argue with
the neighbors. My parents were very vocal. I think it was all "Lies"
or "rumors" about us. Those incidents that burdened my Family
would be the path of trauma that I would go through and endure
with people. At home, I would love to watch cartoons on TV, when

I was taken to a Family friend, "Ms. Carter". She would take care of me. She was very strict and give me "spankings" from time to time as well. My sister Tonya, aged six started attending St. Ann School and Teasie would attend Reid Ross Senior High. She hated that school and she was transferred to E.E. Smith Senior High. She graduated in 1976.

Cartoons and Children's Television shows deeply inspired me. I would love to hear the music of theme songs to Sesame Street, Mr Rogers Neighborhood, The Electric Company and the Uncle Paul Show, a local TV show in NC. It was the music that really hit me. HR. Puff-N-Stuff. The Hudson Brothers Show. The Hot Fudge Show, The Kids from Caper, SPACE:1999, THE SUPERFRIENDS, SHAZAM and ISIS and many others. They were just special to me. Now those shows I just mentioned to you gave me a deep appreciating for music. Vintage Music would blow me away. Tonya and I were glued to our little television that we had 3-4 channels and the screen would be fuzzy and snowy. I remember My father bought a new color Television from GE Appliance in Downtown Fayetteville back in '75 and we got clear TV Picture In our little Den. I, would act out those characters of those TV shows. Especially, "The Hawaiian Punch" commercial. I would try to sing out the lyrics to that song:

"You'll get seven kinds of fruit in Hawaiian Punch" "Seven Kinds of fruit in Hawaiian Punch of that wonderful kind of fruit taste' BOOOMM!'" ZOOM, another television that was shown on PBS. Tonya and I loved it. What we really liked was the shirts the Kids wore. And you know what? My Mother bought shirts like the cast member of ZOOM for both of us." COME ON AND ZOOM-ZOOM-ZOOMA-ZOOMA-ZOOM".

The Captain Kangaroo Show with Mister Moose and the Dancing Bear. Seeing all those wonderful things take me to another world of Childhood innocence. Something I've never experience before. I would act them out. I wanted to be those lovable puppets of those shows. I was just in a world of my own.

We had a 1973 Gray Chevy Impala, that my Dad would drive to work and we as a Family drive to visit his Family, "The Country" and my mother's Family. We had a Stereo set that had a little bar with it. Okay, it had wooden door on top that you lift up. Now, it had a 8-track Tape Player, a little case where you can place your Tapes in. A record player and little bar where you put your alcoholic beverages to the other side. Dad would play records from time to time. Relaxing during the weekend, in our little living room listening all his favorite music artists, Barry White, The O'Jays, The Temptations, The Chi-Lites and Joe Tex. My mother would listen to Al Green, Aretha Franklin and Marvin Gaye. Teasie would buy her records and Tapes, EWF, The Jackson Five, Barry Manilow, Boz Scaggs, Stevie Wonder, Denise Williams and Natalie Cole. Sometimes my parents would dance in our small living room as they listened to the great music of 60's and 70's you must remember, they were young in their early 30's.

St Ann Catholic Church that catered for African-Americans on 357 N Cool Spring Street that started in 1939. It's origins began at a Barbershop call Mack's. Since it was during the Jim Crow period, Father Ryan came to a few African-Americans to help them establish a Church. He confronted some racist construction workers who didn't want to build the church But The Pastor told them to do it right.

St Ann School was established in 1956 for the children of parishioners. It was one of first academic schools to be integrated for boys and girls.

The most impossible subject that I could never summon about that School; Those DAMN NUNS!! (GRRR!) They were characters. Believe me. The nuns were the Daughters of Charity of Emmitsburg, Maryland. These nuns came to honor St Ann School, (the mother of the Blessed Virgin Mary) and to assist and become part of the faculty to serve as teachers and principals during the early 1970's. Subsequently, American military families who were stationed at Fort Bragg and Pope Air Force base sent their children to the school.

The students had to wear uniforms. The boys wore light-blue or white short or long sleeve shirts and dark navy-blue pants. The girls wore white or yellow "Peter Pan" collar shirts and dark blue plaid parochial skirts. It didn't matter what kind of shoes you wore. The students can either wear sport sneakers or dress shoes. In the fall and winter, you wear dark blue or green sweaters. Yet, the point is that as a student of St Ann School. The student must have a cordial, attentive and a presentable appearance.

For Lunch, You bring the steel lunch boxes with a thermist. There were certain style of Lunch boxes of your cartoon character. You must have your phone number tape on either side of your lunch box.

When I started attending St. Ann School, August 1976. I really didn't know what school was all about. That cloudy rainy day, my sister Tonya and I were dropped off that day. I was mostly walking with her as I saw the children running around. Tonya, told me to go to these little kids in line with a nun dress in a snow White Uniform. She had light auburn hair and a gaunt face appearance with piercing blue eyes. She looked liked Karen Grassle. The actress who portrayed the matriarch in the Ingalls Family on the NBC TV series, "Little House on the Prairie". I remembered her because we both took a photo together in May 1975. It was Tonya's first communion. I was so nervous. I just wanted to be with my sister. PERIOD. As this young nun was gathering her new students, we followed her to that little Brick building. I was just walking with the other kids. There was a little office to left of the Hall. But we followed her to the classroom. Again, I was really didn't what was going on. That's when my behavior was kicking in, I would say. The Manic. I was with other kids my age that it highly excited me. I was just a child. As this nun was talking and instructing I was just in a world of kids my age. Sister Janice was so nice that day, we were not there for the whole day. She played some music by Rev. Carey Landry, the HI GOD album and classical music. I was quiet. Okay near the end of that day, Sister Janice had a little knitted bean bag. She tossed to us and we threw the bag to each other. I wanted to play so bad, I wanted to catch the bag and throw it so badly. I was jumping in my chair as my other classmates participating the fun. When one kid threw the bag to me, I caught it and I wanted that kid to throw it back to me. I was enjoying that game. When the day was over, I had to go home,

I frantically searched for my sister. Tonya, nine, was in the Fourth Grade. Her teacher was Mrs. Piltroski.

Now, some of the students had siblings. And most of them had Fathers in the military. The Children were "Military Brats". Their Parents was Stationed on Fort Bragg and Pope AFB. The kids that were in my class, a fairly average class. I remembered a few of them. Jill Pollitt, Carlton Simon, Tyrone Davis, Janice Wallace, Natalie and Nicole Chesnutt (twins), Denise Mitchell, Norman Collins, King Moon, Chris Woody, Louis Williams. A girl named Leticia, Christine Merchen, another girl named Michelle Monk. A kid named Carl. A girl named Danielle and another girl I think her name was Laura. Little did those kids would come to know that this teacher Sister Janice would be a sadistic and a very difficult teacher.

I was physically abused by Sr. Janice in class. The students knew it. They saw it. I had real learning disabilities and I could also remember being dizzy, not concentrating on school work. All those kids that I mentioned definitely knew and saw what happening to me. Especially one. And to this day, If this classmate of mine were to ask about me, this kid would tell the truth about what Sr Janice was doing to me. She was a character. She had no patience with me. I was the only student and a few other that endured her abuse. But I was her toy. As a matter of fact she made an example out of me before the class. My grades were very low and poor. Yet, I was so drawn to the pictures of Jesus Christ from the artwork of Richard and Frances Hook. I was of course, constantly teased in class and by the older students too. By the shape of my Head, I was called, "Pea Head" and my awkward way that I walk, you see I have flat feet. I didn't know who I inherited it from. All the kids really had a ball on me. In some ways, I was like a "clown" talking out loud. Running around in class. Sr. Janice, towards the end, would just let me do my thing. She would SIGH and say, "Travis stop. "Travis look at the board" "Listen to me" "All You cause here is trouble!" "Follow Directions" "Tonya, your little brother is not listening and not paying attention in class" "He's misbehaving in class". Tonya would tell me, "Travis, listen to Sr Janice. Stop doing that". You couldn't stay still!!" Other kids would ask her, "What's wrong with your brother, Tonya? "He's getting into trouble with Sr Janice." Sr. Laura, the principal was just as worse; Verbally abuse towards a highly sensitive child like me. It wasn't all over for me. I had to deal with my Father at home.... I was like being riding in a rollercoaster going up and down.

It was just so terrible for me. A child of six. Even, back in my neighborhood, I was jumped by these kids. I had a BIG WHEEL toy that I would ride around in my back yard. I'll never forget that day. My Dad was outside working on the family car or washing it. Now this was afterschool, I still had on my school clothes. As I rode my BIGWHEEL, in the street. I came across some of the kids near the block corner of the roadside that the pole had the sign of my Street. I can remember one kid just that came towards me and slapped me in my face a few times. A dark skinned little kid had done this. It was like I was attacked by him. I knew his name but I forgot. I tried to block him but I couldn't. I cried and I wept. I think he told me to, "Go Away" "Get outta here". Then I road my BIGWHEEL back home still crying and my Dad just looked at me. He didn't do anything. I went inside the house to our little den and I watched TV, still crying.

At school, I guess you could say that I was a celebrity. I let the kids tease me But I wanted to interact with them. I would wear a "green tobagan" in class. Trying to have that cloth veil Sr Janice has as a part of her uniform. Now mind you, I wasn't the only who had behavioral problems in class. I know there was one kid that wetted in class. I won't mention the child's name. I could never focus in class and as I said earlier, I just thought school was a place for kids to have fun. Well, for me to at least shed some light on those difficult times in my life. I developed a talent in reading. And a deep Appreciation of Biblical Art which to this day still moves me. Now, Sr Janice would teach about the Life of Jesus Christ in artwork By Richard and Frances Hook. The statues at the Church, St. Joseph holding the infant Christ. The virgin Mary with her praying hands wearing dazzling white robes. Adhere to them was the Holy Rosary and a light blue belt on her waist. Her eyes looking up to heaven. Under feet was the serpent Satan as if she defeated him. One of the most pieces of

art, That I still love were the 14 stations of the Cross. My Dad, Tonya
and I would sit at the Back of the small Church. Listening to songs
Spirituals, "O come, O' come Emmanuel". Our pastor Fr Lyons with
his radiant priestly robes. I was magnified by it. He talks about being
good. That Jesus Christ was kind and Loving and He died for our
sins. We would go to church on Saturday evenings at 7pm. Looking
at the statues of Christ. We never missed a day at church during that
time. Never. At, home, we had a small Bible with artwork of Jesus
Christ, I think it was called, HOPE OF THE NATION. I was drawn
to the stories of God and Jesus Christ. Learning to pray. I wanted to
be a priest. Yes, I did. Praying and Helping people. Just being good
as Christ did 2,000 years ago. But of course, My Behavior was like,
"The Looney Tunes" or "Daffy Duck". I just couldn't be still or be
calm for that matter.

At that school, I'll tell you I was the "Celebrity". Just about all the
kids in school knew who I was, "Tonya's Little Brother". So fragile
and highly sensitive. I know during recess, the kids in the playground
would play but I couldn't keep up with them but of course I was
teased. I had one teacher who was fond of me, she would always talk
to me. She was gentle to me. Mrs. Swan, an attractive teacher of
Third grade, she had a big bouffant jet-black hair, a lean slim figured
woman. I would see her and she would tell me just to behave or she
one time looked at me, "If you don't behave yourself, Travis. I'm
going to get me switch and spank you." Though somehow She was
highly fond of me. There was also another teacher that was always
sympathetic and gentle towards me. She had a Marcia Brady flop
Blond hair, I forgot her name. This was the 70's okay! Mrs. Mitchell
and another lady who was always harsh to me because of me running
around the little school house. They were "Den Mothers".

"What's wrong with that kid?" "Can he sit down" "Can he be
still??" I'd run around the school with my light blue or dark blue
pants. My white shirt. Nice little white socks and my Buster Brown
shoes, my parents bought me. All Boys had to wear either White or
light Blue Short sleeved shirts. The Girls would would wear White
or yellow, "Peter Pan" Collar and Tartan dresses. "Hot Dog Day"

was always on Wednesdays for lunch, along with Krispy Kreme Doughnuts. And what you would do is at the beginning of class, you give the lunch money to the teacher or the responsible student would collect the money. It would cost $1.00 for 2 Hot Dogs and 2 Doughnuts. Then the "Den Mothers' would prepare the Hotdogs, boiling them in a big Pot and the aroma of the best chili in the World. Early afternoon, Lunch period would arrive. The student carries the tray of the warmed hotdogs with the would be wrapped in a plastic Merita Bread bag. A bowl of the chili, plastic bottles of red ketchup and yellow mustard, the napkins comes with it. Somehow, the ladies prepared the Lunch very neatly and delicately for the Kids. Mr. Johnson, our Maintenance Man, A very Kind Gentle Man. A big burly man, he was Black. He had a distinctive walk with a deep gruff voice, would bring trays of Milk to the class during lunch.

Then, we had our secretary, Mrs. Franklin. A very pleasing young woman with her generous Southern accent. Her children, Derek (who was in my sister Tonya's class), Damian and Denise (who was in my class) attended. Then there were the Burns and Politts, whom I adore to this day, Michael and Maggie Burns and their little sisters, Jill and little Sarah (who was would attend St.Ann's later). Mrs. Patti Politt was very kind and caring. She and her children was always supportive of me. As you will know, I was a "Celebrity".

The Collins Kids. Rosina, Sivi, (who is my sister Tonya's best friend to this day). Trina and their little brother Norman Lamar (who only attended the school for one year. We had a complicated friendship. Yes, there was a fight between us that Carlton Simon provoked. I remember that day clearly. It was a cold and cloudy day in January 1977. I wore that dumbfounded "green tobagan". Norman took it off my head as Carlton told him to. Then, the fight started, All I knew that Norman apparently slapped me real hard on my Face which had scratched my forehead and I was defenseless. I was crying my head off. Tonya came to me, "Oh Travis!" She took back in school. I couldn't defend myself. My face was bruised and swollen. Norman had heavy hands with nails that left two scratches on my forehead. I was bleeding and crying. Everybody was looking at me. Tonya took me to Sr. Janice who tended my scratches. She washed my face and applied some anointment. Sr. Janice went on a roar at Norman for what he had done to me. "GOD MADE HIM!!" "WHAT IS ONE OF OUR RULES?" Norman replied softly, "Keep your hands to ourselves." "YOU ARE ROUGH!" Norman left crying himself as his sister Sivi walked out of the building with him. That incident to this day scarred me. I will get highly incensed anyone mentioning that to me. But I blame Carlton Simon for inciting that fight. He was known for doing cruel things to kids. Especially to Louis Williams, poor kid, He would just jump him and beat him for no reason. I think that with Norman Lamar Collins, he seemed to be remorseful over the years after that senseless fight. After his Sister Sivi got married, One Friday evening I was at his house. We were Watching, Clint Eastwood's UNFORGIVEN, He lamented that he hated that school and he also saw my symptoms of my Bipolar back then. But I was always there for him. We talked and got along good in High school. I should've stuck with him. But towards the end our friendship was tensed. I can't remember the last time I spoke with him. Yet something in my mind told me to keep my distance from him. Sadly, He passed away awhile back. Yes, I was stricken by it but my sister had told me his health was failing. Lamar was a Body Builder. He was called, "Steroids" in High School. He had 2 kids but I don't know what was the cause of his death. May He rest in peace.

I remained at St Ann School until June 1985. My behavior was off the rack. I was under great emotional stress. I just couldn't simply concentrate on my schoolwork. Yes, I also had to deal with my Family. I would usually get into all kinds of trouble at home. Dealing with my Father. Getting spankings and Whoopins was common for me at the residence of 734 Eufaula Street. Don't talk back. Don't lie. Be a Child! Nuff Said. To be honest, I felt I didn't deserve those strict discipline he imposed on me. Over the time, I was at St Ann, my teachers Miss Lugo and Mrs Smith (more about them later, definitely), would call my Dad from work and have conferences about me of things I done. I'll be honest I was not perfect. But all they would do if I were to behave badly or school work wasn't consistent. CALL

TRAVIS' DADDY. And I got it. No matter what. Even Sean Lane and Vincent Robinson (more about those two, definitely) knew that as well.

Now, I'm not a Family therapist or Child psychologist, harsh discipline and spankings are some ways is not beneficial. It all depends on the Child. ME! I had to deal with school, "Cuttin up" in class. My father instilled the values of raising his three children as his Family had done on him. In my old neighborhood, playing with next door neighbors Craig (Kim) and Carla (Baby Ann) Douglas. Well the Douglas Family were always tolerant of me. And they knew about my parents. Well, I did have a Childhood. We would play around our houses, play Kick Ball in the street. Craig would play Basketball in his Back yard. If not we would throw rocks or chenaberry's and had water fights. But Craig had one undeniable talent. 5 years older than me, He had an ARM. He could throw. He could have been a pitcher and a great Baseball Player. And finally there was Fred. A wild little sprat who lived across the street from my house. He would come play with us. As a sensitive kid sometimes, I think he wanted to fight me all the time. I tolerated him. He was hilarious and smart in school. Craig and Carla had their niece Samantha "Sweet Pea" or "Feebee" would join along. Tonya, would join in with Carla. Yes there were days we would play together and not talk to each other over playing rough or "He say, She say". Me? My Manic self was always into something. In my world, I'd watched TV Cartoons and I would act them out whenever I was alone in my back yard. Playing with the Frogs or Craig would throw dirt rocks at me we'd be in a War or We would get red and black ants and put them in a coke bottle and watch the little insects fight. Craig was a Master at destroying Wasps' nest, Yellow Jackets and honeybees. I do remember he played with a Hornet only one time. "Hornets are Big!", Craig would say. Insects were everywhere at our houses. Hearing Dog Barks. Fire Flies late in the evening when the sun goes down. Now, I was frightened by Dragon Flies but they were harmless. Every summer, the Mosquitoes would have a feast day on us Kids. Getting bitten and having sores "Mosquito bites". Also, hearing those insects whirring during the evening into the night. My father would usually take me to the "Country" to see my cousins. My aunts and Uncles. Having Family get togethers and cookouts. And my Father would reminisce with his siblings about their Childhood and that 'ol house in Eastover. Hearing inspiring stories about my grandparents. Those were the good times.

Back at the "BOTTOM", Craig, Carla and their little niece Samantha, Tonya and I would walk up to the park. Lamon Street Park. Now Tonya and I would have to ask for permission from our parents to go with them. Now, walking to the park or "going to the park" was the main attraction during the summertime because the Park had a 3 Ballparks. There was not only Baseball (Little League) if I may add there was SoftBall by older adults. The Little League had their teams: The Braves (wore white and Royal Blue) uniforms, The Giants wore (Black and White) uniforms, The Cardinals wore (Red and White) uniforms and The Pirates (Yellow and White) uniforms. I played on one team. Boy, I got to tell you more about that.

Also, we would walk to the store on Ramsey Street and buy snacks. First, we had to cross the street. The Cars riding back and forth. We had to be very very careful. Craig, was the ringleader and we would always follow him. I do remember Tonya being a little nervous whenever we did cross the street because she had her little brother to look after.

As you know I went through Dizziness as a Child even before I attended St Ann School. My learning disabilities really took a toll on me. And looking Back, I don't to know how many time that I have to point out or emphasize this. I was in a World. I was a child who wasn't aware of his surroundings. I mostly dream of Fish in an aquarium. Now you might think that this guy is off his rockers talking about this. Fish swimming in an aquarium. They were innocent in a quiet existence. And I think that's what frustrated the Sadistic Sr Janice as she physically abused me. I was already Manic that's for sure. Whenever I listened to music or watch cartoons I was attentive. I developed my urge to read on my own. Again, The Art of the Man From Nazareth. Even, when I was in my church with Dad and

Sister Tonya, my eyes cemented to the statues of Christ during his Passion. To me, that was being good. My fondness was to be an artist. The colorful Art work of Richard and Frances Hook captivated me. Sr Janice would post their Biblical pictures on her board. In my thoughts, Jesus was Good. A great and inspirational man who is the example of all things benevolent. And those paintings were very deep in my heart. My thoughts that Jesus looked like that. Unfortunately, I wasn't attentive in class. At the end of the school day, my sister Tonya, Robin Murphy and I would take a Cab to go home. Our Mean Principal, Sr Laura didn't like that at all. A Cab driver taking us kids home after school. I just thought that school was just a place for Kids to play and mingle. But as for them, Carlton Simon, Tyrone Davis couldn't figure me out. I would run around the playground but whenever I saw my sister, Tonya, I would go to her. During recess, I would go to her and she would say, "Go Travis, Go Travis!" And I would run around.

Every nine weeks would be Report Card Day. It was always held on every Friday. That, late October of 1976, I received my report card. My grades were terrible. I got D's and F's. I was sick that Day, because I was at Miss Carter house I vomited. Poor me. I really didn't know what was going on with me. Later that night at home that Friday evening, My Dad, who was off work, He was a smoker during that time. I remember there was a Halloween Special on TV that featured the Heavy Metal Group KISS. Now, as I was in our little dining room, Dad tried to help me with my homework, He gave me this paper of math problems. Sadly, I couldn't focus and I wasn't paying attention. Dad got up from his chair and smoked his customary VICEROY cigarettes. He walked around the house. I wasn't fully aware of my surroundings.

I was a very very gullible child. Sr Janice would give me basic reading phonics and math books. Or she would just give me work sheets. Again, Sadly, I just couldn't focus. So over the duration at St Ann, in the First Grade, the kids were somewhat against me as well because of my manic demeanor and I think they felt that they could do anything to me. I remember the time she looked at me in the eyes when I was in stuck in Math or phonics, She slapped me in my Face and all the kids in class frozen. She would do that alot to me.

WELLY WELLY WELLY WELL! The kids and the teachers didn't know the problem with this big headed shaped, Flat-footed, wild and couldn't stay still Boy! Wearing that stupid Toboggan on his Head! Take it off your head, You don't wear that in a Classroom!!" What's wrong with him?? He's eating too much sweets! He can't hear! He needs a Spanking. "Travis Did this!" "Travis did that!" "Spank him 'til he's red, black and blue". "HE'S HYPER!" King Moon, Carlton Simon, Tyrone Davis, "It's the mud monster". "He scares me. Let's run". Whenever it came to teasing me and disciplining me. That's the way to do!! "He needs to behave Himself, Tonya!!

At home, I had to deal with the spankings by the "Son of James (PK) McLaurin". Oh Yes, he would help me with my homework if he doesn't bring out a Switch or a Belt. Never liked him helping me with my homework because the next day, Half of the shit is wrong. One time, Sr Janice dragged me from my chair and I was yelling and crying about my Dad helps me with my homework. Sr Janice wouldn't have none of it. Dragged me and just took me to the Coat Cover!! The coat cover is where the kid placed their coats and those metal lunch boxes. I sat on a bench. Pondering with my head down. Feeling so Sad. Yes! He's a kid with serious serious behavioral problems. He needs to be punished!

As the problem child that no one could assimilate at that parochial school. So,instead, he wretch. He could do many many good things. He had a deep discern of the artistry of Richard and Frances Hook. I could draw. I could draw lots of details about the Man 2,000 years ago. So, immersed in Biblical stories. Whenever it came religion in Class. Sr Janice would talk about how we are the Children of God. She always refer God as "God, Our Father", that "God Made you and God made me". Listening to the Music of Rev Carey Landry, the albums she would play on her little record player. She would sing and make us sing. She played Classical music, when we draw or we eat lunch. But if She would get angry at me, I would get sent to the Peace Corner (You're going to Hear alot of that). The Peace Corner is that when your conduct a teacher couldn't deal with you anymore. You're sent to the Principal's Office. Sr Laura, the cruel old little cranky nun of a Woman that's was in her in 60's. A short woman, with gray white-hair, with a saggy wobbly face. Wearing hard rimmed glasses. She looked like the NC Senator Jesse Helms. She did really.

Well, Okay, What else does this "Hyperactive Child" can do? He could read and that's one thing Sr Janice noticed about me. As far the physical abuse that she could afflicted on me. Whenever a kid (especially), in class would tell on me about something I did to him or her. Sr Janice would go on a furor on me. I was the trouble some kid. This little girl named Christine Merschen would always get me in trouble. That I would bite her on her hand. I remember the day. It was a cold rainy. Probably around January or February 1977. All the kids looked at me. HERE WE GO AGAIN!! My classmates were the jury. Sr Janice took me back to the Coat cover and I would sit on the bench. Class proceeded the rest of the afternoon, I would give her cruel looks. So, afterschool was over, Sr Janice wrote a conduct slip on what I did. This was when she said that I needed a "Spanking til I'm red, black and blue!". Sister Janice UGHHH!! As Always, I was feeling bad and crying. Walking with my orange little book bag and my "Pee Wee Kids" Lunch Box. Tonya was outside waiting for me. She saw the sad expression on my Face. I know Tonya was thinking, "Always something with my brother". She asked me, "What's the matter? And I told that I got trouble for biting a girl's hand that I didn't do. Tonya was with her friends. I didn't get spanked that day. I would tell my father what Sr Janice had done to me. But he wouldn't believe me.

I must say this and you can take it to the Bank. Tonya and many others knew what that woman did to me and the students. Sr Janice seemed not to have any realization on the effect on her abusive ways to those students and I.

That time, Sr Janice came to the conclusion about my antics and uncontrolled behavior. She would sigh, shake her head and rolled her eyes upwards. I guess she was thinking, "Let the little creep do what he wants." And I did. There was one time while Sr Janice was having class, the children was attentive. She writing on the Green Blackboard. What I was doing? There was a Piece of paper on my desk and I had a pencil. I was just scribbling. Not doing a thing. Well that was me. I was the pest alright. I didn't seemed to care. Sr Janice did at once wanted me to work with a substitute teacher, ONLY FOR ME! To help me out. I didn't even want it. I remembered I ran around the class. I was in my own world everyone. JUST THE KIDS PERIOD! ALL OF THEM. And they were against me.

Now as a child, I'm speaking and explaining the mind of myself on what I was thinking, feeling and doing. I was 6 years old. I had serious learning disabilities. I looked up to grown ups. Sr Janice, was my teacher I looked up to her and I was fond of her but I hated her abusing me, making a spectacle of me. Just about everyday, Sr Janice would do something to me. Not exaggerating I am not. And of course, at 734 Eufaula Street. I have to deal with Mom and Grand Dad PK's youngest son. Knowing how I was as a Kid at school, I was bullied. I think those Kids just wanted hurt me just for the sake of it. "WELL THAT'S TONYA'S LITTLE BROTHER WHO CAN'T BEHAVE HIMSELF!" I remember even an older girl used to pick on me. I was defenseless when it came to several of the kids picking on me. Several of them felt I deserved it.

I must say this, I wasn't the only child in Class Sr Janice physically abused. Just about several of them. She teased you. She verbally yells at you. But one thing that you don't do, If you have a cold??? Don't sniff your nose! At one time, Norman Collins was yanked from his hand Sr Janice tried to drag him, probably to the Peace corner or the Coat cover. Norman hit her back. She slapped him in the face before. But he wasn't purring up with that. "In the name of God, you don't do that ever", She roared. Poor Louis Williams, She banged his head behind the coat cover. He was crying. Okay, Check this out, Louis was a scrawny kid. I wore that green tobagan in class on my Head because of the Kids popping and hitting my head?? He would wear gloves in CLASS! But Sr Janice Never gave up on me.

January 1977. ABC premiered a mini-series, ROOTS. A saga of an African-American family going through struggles and surviving in America. Based on the Book by the late Alex Haley. He had done a 20-30 year genealogical research from Africa to America. His ancestor slave Kunta Kinte to Chicken George. My Father made Tonya and I watch it. Giving our first glimpse of how Afro-Americans were treated. I didn't understand it. The Racism. The Lynchings . Daddy preached it to us from time to time. We learned and experienced it. I was called a "Nigger" " A Bald Headed Monkey" Hell I was even called, "Kunta Kinte" by this Teenaged White Kid when I was at the YMCA on Fort Bragg Road. We watched all the episodes of that show. It kept re-airing every year. Now, you can watch it on You Tube. Order it on DVD or Blu-Ray. The historic Television event was very very powerful. Then, in 1979, ABC aired ROOTS: The Next Generation. It was continuation of the history of Alex Haley's Family to Jim Crow Era-The great Migration Era and to the Civil Rights Era.

Around this interim, My eldest Sister Gail "Teasie" was attending Methodist College. I would see her from time to time. She looked after her two young siblings. Whatever, My Dad tells her what to do, she would do it. I can go back when I was much younger, there were lots of arguments between my sister and my parents. My mother was very very Vocal, dominant and demanding. Afros were the latest trend and my mother didn't like her eldest daughter having one. Tonya had only Afro-Puffs. You know who would go to Glaspie's Barber shop with his Father and get his customary close crew Hair-cut. Though I didn't like it. But through all those years, it's was my tradition. Life at the residence at 734 Eufaula Street was a regular. My Father working at Kelly Springfield (now Good Year). Few years later my Mother would be there as well. Both of my parents were working quirky shifts. My mother would usually work 2nd shift in the middle of the day. Dad would work 3rd Shift (I hated it when he was on that Shift UGHHH!). But it wasn't until I started attending Terry Sanford Sr. High. They both worked First Shift.

The relationship with my sisters is just a common regular

siblings. We tolerated each other. Teasie would take Tonya to Football games and Band Practices, and take her to movies. Along with her cousin Ashley Burnette. Yeah, our first cousin from my mother's side. He was moody and just mean. He was an awesome Basketball Player. Serious. He was very popular at Methodist College. Our Family thought he was going to be professional. He was just that good.

At School, Sr Janice was still having no patience with me. It seems that Sr Janice was still trying to help me learn. Especially, the CAT test. An examination for all students from the State. I didn't really know what was going on at this time. It tests your aptitude for basic reading and mathematics skills. As for the Students were all ahead of me. Sr Janice was verbally abusive. You have the multiple choice questions in making your answers: Circle it. Multiple Choice: A.B.C.D. I think she never gave me the test anymore. But to top it all off, I have to share this. This was near the end of the 76-77 year. February-March, it was during math class, I was having fear of this woman of what she was doing to me. Constantly Abusing me. Now, this Day, I was doing or at least trying to do my math work. Somehow, I remember I got stuck on some problem. Sr Janice was getting furious with me. She told me, "You're not getting any Lunch until you finish your Work!!!" Then all of a sudden, This Damn Woman picked me up and rocked me like a Baby! "Rock-a-Bye Travis on a Tree top". All the Kids laughed. She was being cruel. I didn't understand what was going on. This is what I meant. She made an example out of me. This Woman went BESERK on me. Then lunch came and of course we say the blessing, "Bless us our Lord. And these are our gifts. Which we are about receive. From our bounty through, Christ our Lord. Amen." And then at the end, Sr Janice said, 'Travis, I care about you too but you have to follow directions." It was something similar to what she was saying to me. My head was down. While the other kids enjoyed their Lunch. I could also remember she scratched me on the back of my ear one day. I told my Father about it. He didn't do Shit!! I guess he felt I deserved it.

My grades were terribly bad. Every nine weeks, when I received my report cards. Again, I didn't know what was going on. Just about every WEEK, Dealing with the stress of being teased and pushed to the ground. I was the VILLAIN. Can He do right for a change?? But that was just the beginning.

On a lighter note, Easter Week, April 1977, there was another TV Mini-Series on NBC, that was just as powerful as ROOTS. Franco Zeffirelli's adaptation, JESUS OF NAZARETH. An all Star international cast starring Anne Bancroft, Michael York, Anthony Quinn, James Earl Jones, James Farrentino, Sir Laurence Olivier, Christopher Plummer, Olivia Hussey, James Mason, Ernest Borgnine and an unknown British actor who is well known all over the world who portrayed Jesus, Robert Powell. I must say this. That series had such a huge impact on me to this day and it does. It premiered on Palm Sunday. My dad watched on our little new TV from Major Appliance, I think I was so excited maybe it was on impulse that I had to watch it. And me wearing my little t-shirt and my little underwear, Dad made me watch it. At school, It was the talk of the town, I remember pulling out a scrap out of a TV guide and I showed it to Sr Janice was touched as she was talking to Sr Laura about it. Apparently, they watched it. I really think that Sr Janice knew how much that TV Movie meant to me. And today, 2021, It is still a powerful popular Iconic film. It was shown on NBC in 1977, 1978, 1979, 1980, 1984, 1987 and 1990.

A lighter note, I was slowly catching on in class of what Sr Janice was teaching me. It was near the end of the School year. St Ann School always had Plays for school at the Social Hall that was recently completely constructed. It was an Easter Play that focused on the Passion of Christ. I was there that evening. The spring of 1977 was beautiful. The green lawn blossoming. With soft little dandelions blossoming on the playground on 365 N. Cool Spring Street. The honeybees getting their grub on the little green clover flowers so they make the real Honey. To much to her suprise, Sr Janice was noticing that I was finally learning my schoolwork. I do remember that she said to me like, "Travis, Jesus is going to help you". Much to my suprise, I felt like she was giving me hope. And she gave me a delightful smile. My reading was improving and things was slowly progressing for me.

St Ann's Bazzar, an annual Social event that always held on the first Saturday of May. It was like a carnival for the kids from each Grade to play and perform. Arts and Craft. Live Music. Yes, A live Band that would play music. Food being cooked and Grilled. I think the purpose for that event was to raise money for the School. Well, As for me, I enjoyed it. Just about everyone in your Class attended. Yes, the Nuns too and a few from St. Patrick's School. Though, I acted like a Clown of myself most of the times but I really enjoyed them indeed.

As you know, when there's a beginning of a School Year. There's always the end. By the time, I was finally catching on learning of what's going on in school. I do remember that last Day in School in June. I was given my report card. All, the Kids were excited that School was over and the summer was straight ahead. Still, I didn't know what was going on. Except for Sr Janice, towards the end as I was making a little progress. She came to the conclusion that I wasn't ready for the Second grade. I was held back. I failed the First Grade year, 1976-1977. I was to return to St Ann later that August of 1977. The Next School year, I would be prepared. It would be new, different and most off all, I would mingle and socialize a new special group of Children who had deeply inspired me. They put a light in my eyes.

As to explain this, is that during my first year attending was very traumatic, painful and fruitless. I had no motivation to learn and I only thought that Going to school was just being with the Children. Now, I was wasn't the only child that Sr Janice held back. She failed a few others. As for my Classmates, Jill Pollitt, Carlton Simon. Tyrone Davis, Michelle Monk and the rest were more academically ahead of me. I was so much of a burden to them. I just didn't understand. It reached to the point that I was the "VILLAIN". I didn't know exactly what to do my First Year at that school. And those kids knew and saw what that Nun had and put me through. I would be "DAMNED" if they were to lie and say abruptly. "Sr Janice didn't do that to

Travis". They will deal with me PERSONALLY. I didn't deserved to be physically and verbally abused. My self-esteem was already low. Depressed and the Mood Swings was present. PEOPLE!! Lend me your ears! I was just a Child. It would follow me to this day even thinking about it. Despite all the ingredients of Bipolar Disorder, I inherited from my Mother, it come into full display at St Ann School.

SUMMER OF '1977

The summer was always playful and cheerful in "THE BOTTOM". The summer, the kids were taking their break. The neighborhood was always people talking loud. Or you could hear the latest Soul music blasting in someone's speakers or houses. The Kids riding their bikes. The Echoes of Dogs Barking constantly. Whirring of insects, the fireflies and cricketts. The Flashy Cars driving through the Street of Eufaula. People socializing, talking loud. Grilling and Barbecues. Neighbors bickering and fussing with each other. Eufaula Street was a long strip. Just a long strip. The Brothers washing and waxing their Cars down. Or you would just go to the Lamon Street Park. My Oldest Sister, Gail, "Teasie" or "Possum", was looking exemplary very attractive. Oh Yes, My sister had guys chasing after her. Tonya?? Well, she was just growing up. Now, everyone tells me and compliment how attractive my older sisters are. Summer was much fun for us when our neighbors the Douglas' kids, Craig (Kim), Carla (Baby Ann) and little "Sweetpea" looking like the lovable Snoopy from Peanuts. But, at our house, when Dad is relaxing in his new pull out couch and watching TV and my Mother was either at work during the second shift. Teasie would help Mom in the kitchen cook dinner as Tonya would look on. As I was running and playing as a Kid. Teasie would have her 8-Track Tapes play them on our Stereo. She would take Tonya along with her adventures. Meeting some of her friends from High school. We had a little dark-Green Chevy Car Along with the 73 Impala. Now this summer, when I watched TV, I saw a footage something like Bursting fire crackers in Space, a Robot and a Blonde haired looking kid. I definitely couldn't figure it out. Little did I know that Clip on TV would be a milestone in the History of Tinsletown. A phenomenon was already taking place. So, that summer and the ones that followed, I lived in my own world. Playing the Heavy Metal group KISS in my sisters little room, I knew at St Ann's. from Carlton Simon, I would wander around the house. Tonya and I would play in our backyard as Craig would start rock fights with us. Carla, who just turned six would be attending school later that year. We would have to get to the house after playing outside because of the Mosquitoes were having a feast on our arms and legs. The Alabamian, fast talking and gentle Mr. Henry Douglas, Craig and Carla's father would love to see his large Garden Blossoming, Cabbage, Large Corn Stalks. You would just see GREEN. Everywhere. All kinds of vegetables. Their Mother, (Mrs Douglas) would go out to the front yard to her porch with her bowl and have her green peas. We would help peel them. They didn't mind me. But Craig HATED getting his hair cut by his father. Having a Fade looking very like he was going to boot camp. Their sisters, Cathy "Sister" as they would call her and the grouchy, non smiling Debbie would do the chores around their house as I was just having a time of my life! I WAS KID. And I just turned seven.

My father would take us out to the "Country". "We're going to the country", he would say. Eastover, Stedman, to visit his Family, his Siblings, Uncle D or "DW", Aunt Christine, Aunt Lois and Aunt Bronnie, My Dad's eldest Brother, "Uncle MAC" would come from Portchester, NY. And a crew of my cousins would come play with us. We had fun. The same with my Mother's Side, Sundays was always visiting Grand Ma Daisy at the little shack house, that still exists Today and the Elizabeth A.M.E Zion. I always asks myself, "How did my Grandmother Feel, about having a Full Brood of Children of 14, and Grandkids running around everywhere?" But that was her Family.

That summer was something of a benediction for me. A time to mend.

St Ann School - August 26, 1977

It was a cool sunny blue morning. Teasie dropped Tonya and I off to school. All the kids were running around the playground. I was walking past the kids looking around. And then, I recognized some of the kids from my class earlier that year. I was looking around still didn't know where to go. But it was not until I heard a familiar voice calling my name. "Travis!" "Travis!" "Travis!" Over here. Come here. You're over here!" It was Sr Janice flashing a bright smile. She was dressed in her regular nun's attire. She was wearing a pure white dress, with her black stockings and black shoes. The nuns would later wear Dark Navy Blue Uniforms in the Fall and Winter. Calling my name, her hand was waving to me come to her. Then I realized that I was going to have this woman again as my teacher. But I was nervous and I didn't know what to do. All the kids were forming lines as the teachers were getting them to a straight line. I was silent. Then I got in line with these new kids that was already in line ready to walk behind Sr Janice in the building for the first day of school. I was thinking to myself, "I know this place. I've been here before". Then Sr Janice and all the new registered kids walked behind her to the classroom. I know this, I was thinking to myself. To my astonishment, I was in the same classroom earlier this year. I know this place, though I was quiet. Still nervous. All the kids went to the desks and sat down. "I know this place." I was thinking to myself. These were new kids in my class. But I kept quiet. I saw all the alphabets, numbers and the decorations Sr Janice must have done to prepare for her new class. I just took a seat and sat down. Then,

Class Began. Sr Janice, then took her roll call on her pad and pen. Roll Call. She called our names and we had to respond "Here!".

When, it came to me, Sr Janice called my name, "We know you already," as she smiled. Now some of the kids didn't show up yet and they were late. As I was looking everywhere in the classroom. Nervous and quiet. "I know this place". I just couldn't get a grip of what was going on.

Until, class began. We did the routine. I knew about that too. Then, as I was sitting quietly on my desk with the new students, this small little girl, out of the Blue just started talking to me. She knew my name already. Now, this girl had a gentle, angelic appearance. She had dark-brown olive skin complexion. Short dark Brunette Hair and innocent brown eyes. She sensed that I was nervous. She was just reaching out to me. I'd be proud to say that this little girl healed me that morning. Her name was Michelle Balsamo.

Sr Janice wanted me to give some paperwork to Miss Williams (now Mrs McDonald), the second grade teacher next to our room. Much to my suprise, when I knocked on the door, there were kids that were in my class earlier that year. "HI TRAVIS!!!" they all said. I remembered that I didn't smile at them but I just looked at them. They seemed overjoyed to see me despite what Sr Janice had done to me. And then I realized that everything was slowly coming together for me. Since it was a short day, some of the students showed up late for the class. A boy and a girl, who were "Twins", as Sr Janice has said. They were April and Forrest Alvarez. Now, there was another student that came late to class, was a cherub girl with short dark brunette hair and rosy cheeks. She was wearing this dark green ruffled shirt and of course she was wearing bell bottoms. With nice white socks and sandals. I remembered this girl saying proudly, "I'm happy to be here!" Her name was Sheri Garvin.

So, I guess I can say that day went very good for me. Only, I knew that I was going to have to deal with Sr Janice again with a new class. But, academically, I was catching on quick. Of course, I was teased that I was in first grade. "Travis Flunked the First grade.' You're a

The Gift

Flunker!" It really bothered me. Tonya was defensive of me, telling them to leave her little brother alone.

Before, I continue, I must say this, as these new classmates of mine were different. Whenever it came to me, they all rooted for me. Some came and left partly because most of them they were "Military Brats". Their father's were stationed in Fort Bragg or Pope AFB. For the next eight years these kids became a vital point in my life. April and Forrest Alvarez, Stephanie Blackburn, Robbie Ankrim, Michelle Balsamo, Genevieve Beateau, Ronald Bowling, Angela Butler, Myra Call, Ann E Carpenter, Jenny Chriss, Loretta Dempsey, Shannon Davis, Tracy Desert, Jennifer ?, Kenny ?, Steve Eden, Danielle A Ely, Alexandra Ewing, Chris Keith Franklin, Sheri Garvin, Kelly Giles, Jamie Lewis, Charlotte Hales, Morgan Kelly Hardwick, Ricky Holmes, Allyson Hood, Cynthia Horner, Lori Hoskins (miss you always), Carol Kramer, Kevin Jones, Sean Lean, David Lee, Shawana Davis, Shenikka McNeil, Mark Michel (my Boy), Kim Micheaux, Tommy Miller, Michael Ortiz, Lance Prescott, Jennifer Rathke, Phillip Raymond, John Rice, Allyson Robinson, Vincent Robinson, Andy and Jack Seckley, Derek L Sellers, John Senninger, Julie Shanabruch, Lorena Marie Shepard, Juliet Smith, Don Spears, Teddy Swift, Maurice A Thomas, Julie Trevino, Matthew Vaughan, Janice Wallace, Jason Weeks and Ivy M Wright.

I established great Friendships with them. They were children who were just innocent. We were a Gang. I belonged to them. Only eight of them, along with me, graduated from St Ann School in June 1985.

The memories will always be forever cherished in my heart. It will never be erased. We watched each other grow up and we knew our ways. We had our cliques, Believe me. But we had a bond, a loyal bond. We believed in each other and supported each other. We had our days when we teased each other. Being tolerant of each other. Over those years, my interaction with them was never flawed. It built my self esteem. As, being, "THE GIFT" proves that on December 1983.

As the school passed on that year, somehow I was more calmed more than ever before. Then as the days went on, I was mostly quiet and kept mostly to myself. Little did everyone know, I was studying my new classmates and getting acquainted with them. Julie Shanabruch and Lorena Shepard. Just about everything was sort of looking bright for me. During this time, I forged a friendship with this skinny scrawny, white blonde haired kid, his name was Mark Michel. During this interim, a phenomena had already begun. A Science Fiction film was changing Hollywood Cinema, I'd be proud to say that I was a part of it. STAR WARS: EPISODE IV: A NEW HOPE was released in May 1977. Mark was a true Fan. He had a STAR WARS lunch box . He always talked about it. It was the talk at the school. Around September-October, we moved our desks and chairs to arrange the class. But I was so drawn to this kid. As we moved our desks Sr Janice had us doing. I sat next to him. We gave each other "Gimme Fives" I remember and we kind of embraced that day. We were friends officially. But I never forgot the kids that I was in class with earlier that year. I knew them and they knew me. I still tagged along with them. I guess since I was held back, Jill Pollitt, Tyrone Davis and few of the other kids were sympathetic to me after the Hell Sr Janice put me through.

As, I was getting older, my behavior was still unruly but I could contain myself. Hey! I was in a class with new students. And finally having Friends. I was always glad to see Mark. Mark Michel and Steve Eden played along before I came into the picture. It was fully understood that Tonya's little Brother was finally catching on in school. To me, that really didn't matter to me.

A behavior Pattern ensued. All the symptoms were there no doubt. But over the years as I was there it was slowly becoming conspicuous to the teachers and my classmates. Like a Rollercoaster, I would say. It was a load, a heavy burden off me that Sr Janice was noticing my improving progress in school. And as well as my Friendship with Mark Michel. She couldn't break that. She knew that I had a friend. A skinny scrawny child, barely wearing clothes my size, my classmates, knew me already.

Michelle Balsamo, Julie Shanabruch and Lorena Shepard was

always attentive. They always encouraged me. I would blow "kisses" to Sheri Garvin and her face would jump in suprise and of course she would tell on me. Mark and I would do our best to chase the Girls around the playground. But I was still being teased as "The Flunker". That was still really bothering me. Being introverted, I couldn't defend myself and from time to time the kids would still thump me on my head. But my Friendship with Mark was more important to me than anything else. Yes, He got me hooked on STAR WARS. He would draw little pictures of the spaceships. "Star Wars is BAD!" said Robbie Ankrim.

During that time, I was invited to parties. The first one was by Chris Woody, He passed to the second grade. It very kind of him that October. I was so excited that I remember that he gave me my number And I would call him all the time. The party was mostly boys, Carlton Simon, Tyrone Davis, Louis Williams and a few others. Back then, you can trust your child to give them to your friend's parents to chaperone.

Another memory in my life was one of the most enjoyment ever. Going to the Movies to see STAR WARS (Star Wars: Episode IV: A New Hope). I do remember it. A chilly, cold Friday evening and it was shown at the Cross Creek Mall Cinema around November-December 1977. I was really really excited because that was the talk at the School. Mark would bring his action figures and talk about it and make funny special effects sounds with his mouth. That was a treat. I don't know what made my Father take Tonya and I to go see it but it was very very special. The Mall was a small shopping center that just opened. I saw the lights when we arrived at the theater. The Movie Poster Ads were in front of the theater. We were dressed warm in our coats. Dad purchased the tickets. I remember walking to the poster of George Lucas' Sci-Fi Film. I was nervous at first glancing at the movie poster. The farm Boy Luke Skywalker raising his Lightsaber with all his might and strength. The lovely Princess Leia looking sexy with a bad attitude look with a laser gun. And the evil Darth Vader presence in the background. My eyes popped. I knew that I was into something special. Dad treated us to everything.

Popcorn and Coke. There was hardly anyone in the theater that night. It was pitched black. Dad guided us to sit in the center not far back. I never left my seat. My attention and my eyes were glued to the large Silver Screen. It was something a child could never forget and Again I must say that I'm gracious to be a part of that popular culture. A Great cinematic Experience.

Do you remember your favorite STAR WARS character. Me? Luke Skywalker. Then on Saturday Mornings you see Commercials of the Star Wars Action Figures. Since Christmas was approaching, I thought for sure I would get them. Though I couldn't pronounce, "The Millennium Falcon."

So, we were doing artwork in class one day. Sr Janice, occasionally, would put on a little music. Rev Carey Landry and classical music. What we were supposed to do that day was to make cards of the Three Wise Men. What you had to do was place your thumb on an ink plate. Press it on a card and get your red marker. And draw a crown on it. Ivy Wright and I were both working together but I couldn't really press my thumb because it smeared. Ivy was doing it correctly. Sr Janice saw me doing it incorrectly and She just went BERSERK! She took my hand violently to press my thumb on the Black ink plate. This Woman was returning to her old ways. Now, Ivy was just looking because she was already physically abusive to her cousin Derek Sellers, Tommy Miller and Kowalski Plummer. Those were her new targets. Then all of a sudden, That Damn Woman took my arm and wrestling and pulling it back. And that Shit hurt. I was crying. Crying my eyes out. And she roared, "Go to the Bathroom!" I was shaking and slowly, I went to the Boys room, I walked to the corner of the wall and the sink. Weeping and Weeping. As I had my head down, Michael Burns entered and he saw me crying with my head. Of course, you know, I was well known to most of the kids at the school. Michael approached me.

"Travis?" he said softly. I didn't answer.

"What's the matter? What's wrong?" I didn't answer. Shaking and I could barely talk.

"Did Sr Janice do anything to you? " asked Michael. I was feeling pitiful and I told Michael what she had done. "Sr Janice did that to you?" Michael Burns had a furious look on his face. And he walked out of the Boys room.

Flu Season arrived. The Kids were getting sick. I don't know how I got it. Lorena Shepard, poor Lorena's dress vomited by Jamie Lewis. He had to leave that day. Before the Christmas school break, one morning or late night, at home I experienced the worst WHOOPING COUGH ever in my life. Since our little room we only had two Beds so I slept with Teasie. I vomited the day before. It was unbearable. I didn't attend school that day. My sister was comforting me as I was constantly sounding like one of the cartoon characters I watched on Saturday mornings. I didn't attend school anytime that weekend because I was stricken with influenza.

Christmas 1977 was on a Sunday. I was sick though. "Travis, look what you got", said an excited Tonya as she presented me with THE GREEN MACHINE. I had a GI-JOE figure and a Spider-Man Toy Kit. [I loved Spider-Man. He was my favorite and still is my Comic Book Hero.] Thanks to THE ELECTRIC COMPANY. I barely play my toys, I remember but I just stayed home. Recovering from the flu.

January 1978. A new year. Classes resumed at St Ann's. Most of the kids brought some of their toys to class. I didn't bring any of mine. Feeling better from that miserable flu. The weather in Fayetteville was getting An Ice Storm. I don't remember school had to close but it very bad, indeed. But, Mark Michel and I were inseparable. Mark would try to sing songs he knew. Especially, "BRICK HOUSE" by the Commadores and this other song which would be one of the most Rock-N-Roll Classic. "We will Rock You/We are the Champions" By QUEEN. I was supposed to spend the weekend at his house near Fire Fox, A Military neighborhood. Now Mark's mother and my sister Teasie talked about it. Mark's Mother didn't have a problem with it. The plan was that Friday, I remember Teasie was to have my bag prepared. I was so excited. The next day, I told Sr Janice that I was going to Mark's house. She was glad and told me to be careful. Mark's mother was waiting in her car. Waiting for my Sister. Teasie never showed up. UGHH!! Mrs Michel couldn't wait any longer. The Ice Storm still effected Fayetteville. Extremely cold. But, when I got to his house, with school book bag, Mark went to the living room and he turned on the stereo and played the radio. I didn't do anything but let Mark run the show. He showed me his room. It was nothing But STAR WARS galore. He had just about every toy. A Tie fighter and X-Wing fighter was hanging from the roof. I was mesmerized. I met his Father, A kind, Friendly Man. Then as time passed it was time for me to go. Mrs Michel wanted to make sure that I was safe at home. She called my father and told him everything's alright. She had to take me home. But I had to deal with my Father and I was certain I was going to get a whoopin but I didn't. When Mark and his mother dropped me and left, I went through the door, My Dad was standing by our new fireplace, waiting. He just expressed his worry and why I didn't wait for Teasie but He didn't do anything to me. The plan was we were going to see STAR WARS and spent the night at his house but that never happened. Now, Mark had a sister, Janice and two older Brothers. Ever since, Sr Janice warned us to stop teasing Michelle Balsamo and Julie Shanabruch, we were Boys. She sensed it. Travis was becoming more sociable. Academically, improving there was no stopping. I saw STAR WARS and we both talked about it along with Steve Eden and Andy Seckely. Sr Janice was becoming proud of me.

Later that month, Carla Douglas, my next door neighbor, invited me to her Birthday Party at her house. Several of the Kids from the "BOTTOM" she invited. I attended another party. The Douglas' were already tolerant of me as I explained earlier. They served Ice cream and cake. Craig was nowhere to be seen. Carla's niece, Samantha "Sweet Pea" "Snoopy", she was just only three years old. One thing I do remember was that photo we all took together. I still think she has it.

As the months passed into the Spring, things was looking good for me. And as I Catholic, I attended Church regularly. But there were Things I knew that I could do. I could draw. The Biblical Art work of Richard and Frances Hook. At class, When Sr Janice put on the music of Rev. Carey Landry, We all sung together. I like the Crayola Crayons, because whenever we drew pictures, we would have to create a story. I'd like doing that. I just love Art.

St Ann's Bazzar, May 1978, was held. I was so excited that I got my Face painted like Ace Frehley of the rock Group KISS. Everybody was there. I remember Carlton Simon had his face painted like Peter Chriss. Now, on this particular Day, Each class has to do a presentation. Tonya, A fifth grader and her class had to present, Snow White and the Seven Dwarfs. Their teacher was Mrs. Polumbo, an attractive woman. They had to make Puppets with socks and do the dialogue. Tonya was "GRUMPY". My sister was Funny as HELL! I laughed during the whole performance but it was FUNNY. You just had to be there. A live Band was there. They did a cover of, Steely Dan's "Peg". My Hyper Manic self was running everywhere. When I came home that day, I had to wash off the face paint makeup because Dad wasn't having it. I was just a child. No harm.

To the end of the school year, as my grades improved. Again, Sr Janice was proud. Then one day in class, there was another nun that came and visit us. All of kids sat on the floor and We were singing songs. It was all good and lovely. Since, Sr Janice noticed that I could sing. She let me do my own thing. They were bugging out on me. Along with Mark Michel, John Rice, Lance Prescott (who was the tallest in our class.Those long legs he had). He could run. Fast.

*I finally got Sheri Garvin this time. Sr Laura and Sr Janice were both in class. As you know, I would get in trouble for blowing kisses at her. She didn't like it. I took Sheri's hand and she became my dancing partner and I did something of a Flamenco Dance. They Laughed so hard. I knew Sheri didn't like that but it was my way of chasing her. GOTCHA SHERI.

In June 1978, I received my report card and I was promoted to the Second Grade. Sr Janice never returned to St Ann's again.

The Summer of 1978. This summer was different. My parents signed Tonya and I to attend the YMCA on Fort Bragg Road. (That was not until the summer of 1979). There were some students that attended St Ann's that went there. Especially, this Kid named Brad. He was in the 3rd grade. He was a dorky, freckled face and had red hair. His Body was shaped funny and he had issues. He would bully me around and threaten me. At school, none of the Kids liked him. He really didn't have any friends except this kid named Mark. Tonya and I were there. Yet, She would protect me from some of the students of St Ann's because, "I flunked the First Grade". And I was getting tired of that shit. I told them to leave me alone. Leonard Hill was something of a ringleader calling me a "Flunker". The YMCA was giving Swimming lessons and I wanted to learn how to swim. So, my mother signed Tonya and I to swimming lessons. It was just that I was so happy that I was in the pool and I couldn't concentrate. The instructors were worried about me because of depth of the pool. They were certain that I was not ready to reach to the 9th Feet. Tonya caught on quick. It was just like I was so happy to be in the water with Kids. Yet, a few of those lifeguards were watching me. I attended the YMCA in the summers of 1979, 1980 and 1981. Only Tonya never returned.

My rollercoaster behavior was slowly coming to notice to the kids at School. My 2nd grade teacher, Miss Williams (now Mrs McDonald), was okay. A fairly attractive Woman in her late twenties I mean she would get on me from time to time. As my Friendship with Mark still blossomed, she separated us. She was radical to an extent about being "Black". I never really had any issues with her. She would give us Spankings. It was through her that she began teaching us about the Slain Civil Rights Leader. An Apostle of nonviolence. The Reverend from Atlanta, Georgia since it was the 10th anniversary of his Assassination. Mark, Steve Eden and I were talking about this new STAR WARS Rip off Spoof TV show on ABC called BATTLESTAR GALATICA. Also, there was a TV Special that was shown on NBC, THE KISS MEETS THE PHANTOM later that October around Halloween. We had new students added to the bunch. A new nun came to the First Grade after Sr Janice left. A tall woman in her late thirties, with big frame, hard rimmed dark brown glasses. Very direct but she was a "Nun of reason". Her name was Sr

Saundra. She prepared us for Catholic Church and for Penance. April Alvarez and Julie Trevino became the best of Friends, 'THELMA AND LOUISE'. But there was a short Black kid that was a grade ahead of me and he was in our reading class. A little round face with a square-shaped head and he wore hard glasses with a fade haircut. I don't think he ever got a hair cut as I did. I was drawn to him because he could run real fast with his short stocky legs and he had "beady" little eyes with a high-pitched voice. He quickly made friends but he always had to prove himself. His name was Vincent Robinson. The older kids would call him, "Little Man". He loved Sports I could tell. He would play with Lance Prescott and They both got along well. It took awhile for Vincent and I to clique. Well, He really didn't care too much for me at first. We had a fight one time where we both got the best of each other. He could handle himself. Another Kid named Ricky Holmes, He was a character. He was built for his size. He was very mischievous than I. Still, I was the Hyper-Manic overly sensitive kid just to remind you. Talking excessively and getting sent to the "Peace Corner". The peace corner was primarily an office and you sat to a desk near the Secretary office, Mrs Franklin and you get briefed by the Principal who was Sr Laura. That Christmas 1978, I finally got my STAR WARS toys what every kid would wished for. And a Red Buckroo Bike. Also, in December, my father took Tonya and I to see another Cinematic Experience for us, Richard Donner's SUPERMAN: THE MOVIE. It was crowded at the Cross Creek Cinema at the Mall.

Listening to Music was another hobby I enjoyed. The only two radio stations in Fayetteville were WFLB 140am and WIDU 1600am. WIDU was the Black radio station that played Soul and R&B. WFLB played variety of music. Yes, indeed. The Disco scene. Back at the residence of 734 Eufaula Street. My parents added an extra room and they had to arrange the house. The Den was added and a fireplace as I pointed out earlier, Tonya and I were growing up. Teasie still attending Methodist College. As all Children, I had to sleep in the dark in my room. Scared of the Dark. I never had any Nightmares. But somehow, I fell asleep.

1979

Sr Saundra was getting us prepared for our First Communion. But, that April, She carried out a play for us getting our Penance. Penance was the sacrament where you confess your sins to your Catholic Priest then after that you recite the Act of Contrition. In conclusion, the priest gives prayers saying 3-4 Hail Marys or Our Fathers. Our play focused on Zacchaeus the Tax Collector. It was only for the ones who were Catholic in our Class. So Sr Saundra gave us a script and We would read and practise. I remember playing Jesus. John Rice was Zaccheus. Michelle Balsamo was the narrator. Then there was another girl who took part in the play. Her name was Jennifer. A delightful little chubby girl with light auburn hair. It was held on a Saturday morning, Beautiful Spring Day, My mother came with Tonya and I to the ceremony that day. We had to perform in front of our Family at the church, I was nervous, of course. It went swell and Our Pastor, Father Lyon explained and emphasize on the importance of giving, not being selfish and about the story of the Tax Collector.

St Ann's Bazzar- May 1979. A Beautiful Sunny Day. All Fun and Games. Every Class had to perform musical or play. My Class had to the "HOKEY POKEY". Mrs McDonald had us doing the dance. The Boys had to be gentlemen to the girls to be our dancing partners. Jennifer was my partner. She wore a springy dress like "Dorothy" of THE WIZARD OF OZ. All the Boys had to be nice to the Girls. We performed the dance routine. I took her hand and she twirled around being an innocent girl. Doing the "HOKEY POKEY". Julie Trevino's mother had a food stand and making delicious Tacos. A very nice Lady. Julie was a Tomboy and Tough. April Alvarez and I fought one time but Julie was the exception. She hated dresses she told me one time. Well that was the dress code for the girls in school. She came from Corpus Christi, TX. I think she had 2-3 older Brothers and older sister, Edna, who was in my sister Tonya's Class. The St. Ann's Bazzar was like the Historic music festival in Bethel, NY back in 1969. Not close to it. No way near it.

First Communion arrived. Sr Saundra had us making ribbons of the Holy Cup and the circular White waifer of Christ the day prior. I was getting nervous. That, Saturday morning in May, My Family was getting ready for this Special religious event. I wore a little dark blue suit with a brown clip on tie. We had to arrive at the Church early so that the Nuns can arrange us in a line to go to the Social Hall were it was held. The girls were looking lovely with their white dresses. I was cutting up as Hell. Me and this Kid were just laughing in class. When it was time for all the children to go to the Social Hall. We walked out of the school. Sr Saundra and a few nuns were chaperones. And Damn it, there was a Bad foul smell. I think it was the sewer. "It stinks" I said and I was clowning around. All of us in line were walking slowly to the Social Hall to receive our First Communion. Dad took some pictures with the Family Camera but it didn't come out good. I received my First Communion from Fr Lyon, May 12, 1979.

Mark Michel was talking about going to Florida during this time in class. He was so excited. I was just thinking that he was going to return. But He wasn't joking. The majority of the kids at school had to relocate because they were, "Military Brats".

June 1979 – the last Day of school and our report cards were given. I was promoted to the Third Grade. I saw Mark running to his mother's car and he got in. I never heard from him again. It was a Special Friendship between Mark and I. NO! Race has nothing to do with it. Don't get me started. Along with him, John Rice, Andy Seckley, Michelle Balsamo, Julie Shanabruch (who left early that year because her family was stationed at another military Base). Mark Michel really made me open up more though I was an introvert and behaviorally unruly. We both got in trouble together. We were innocent little children just enjoying life. Over the years, Mark was on my mind but I always had a feeling that I was going to hear from him again. That was put to rest for the next 23 year later.

Summer 1979. My neighborhood, "THE BOTTOM" was going through another hot summer. People talking loud. Dogs Barking. Craig, Carla, my sister Tonya and I were just being kids. You have to ask Mom and Dad if they would give you their permission to go to the Park. Walking to the Park was like a long walking From Eufaula Street to Lamon Street Park. Watching the little league play Baseball. The ice cream Man would come and that excited us. A few of the Kids hated us when we got our treats. We could afford it. But this summer was different. Tonya and I had to get our tonsils surgically removed. When Tonya got hers removed unfortunately she had a very bad allergic reaction. She vomited Blood and she was rushed to the Hospital. Tonya had to stay home for the remainder of that summer. First, she fractured her arm at a roller Skating Rink and now this. I vaguely remember that night. Mom and Dad were walking hurriedly through the house. Teasie had to stay home and watch after me. When they returned home, because she was still sick, Tonya wore her white pajamas around the house.

Then it was my turn. Late July-early August, My mother took me to the Highsmith-Rainey Hospital to get checked in. I was nervous of course. Actually, I wasn't supposed to be there but under Otolaryngologist Dr Butler's strict orders, he wanted me there at that Hospital. But the aftermath was I would enjoy some good ice cream. As I got there, I was taken to my room, there was an older kid who could've been in his late teens that was there. But he and his mother were very kind and generous to us. All I knew, I had my pajamas given to me to wear and stay in bed. That young kid and I got along great. The TV was there and we watched the upcoming shows as the night came.

I was running my mouth as we watched TV. I remembered we watched an episode of THE OUTER LIMITS and a few shows. The second Day, he was discharged and I had my tonsils taken out.

A nurse carrying a tray had a syringe and I had to get an injection on my butt. OWW! That hurt. Then I was taken to the operating room. Still laying on the bed looking everywhere, the nurses were walking around. They kept me company. "How are you, Travis?" I was talking talking, talking and talking. I think I had to get an IV because this guy was sticking this damn needle in my left hand. I think he was trying to get a vein. So, as I was prattling, a black circular mask put gently on my nose and mouth. Then a BLACK OUT.

I woke with a pain down in my throat. Coughing and Spitting up Blood. I was asking and crying for my mother, "MAMA! MAMA! She was there with me as they rolled me back to my room. Teasie and Tonya came to visit me. They bought Mom some lunch. "Ewww, you're spitting up blood" said Tonya as she put a container to my mouth. I couldn't talk anymore. Mom and Dad had to take turns coming to the Hospital to watch over me during the night. One Night in particular, Dad was watching TV as I was rolled to the other side of the room where that young man was. He was watching a Film about some teen agers hanging out. But I remember the film starred Ron Howard (from Happy Days), but there was a song at the end of that film that l like by the Beach Boys. The Next Morning, Dad was gone. I was getting scared so I got up from my bed and walked out my room. The Receptionist knew my name and they told me that my father was gone. Mom came later that Day. So, I was discharged and I was going home.

Now that I was home, I experienced the most agonizing painful ear aches. So painful, tears were coming down my eyes. That was one effect of my throat healing from that surgery. UGH! Anyway, I was glad that I was home. The days of summer past. I was getting better. That August, I had to get ready to return to school.

AUGUST- 1979

After recovering from my tonsils surgery. I was a little moody. I hardly attended school the first day. But I do remember, it was on a cloudy day. Tonya was in the 7th grade. Teddy Swift. A really silly kid. I was playing with him on the playground. Then another kid started talking to me. His name was Kenny. A Puerto Rican child from NY, I believe. He had a Sister who was in a Grade ahead of my sister. Now Back to my socializing with this Kid. I hardly spoke to him. Okay, He wasn't involved in this But somehow, Teddy and I were spitting at each other. Teddy has this laugh which will make you laugh. We were spitting at each other and I was getting mad at him. I know that I got him a couple of times as we were spitting at each other. Of course, the nuns were chaperones that morning. My Third Grade Teacher was Mrs Ann Ortiz, Michael's mother. Yes, he was a cute youngster. He favored his mother's looks. His father, worked at the Kelly Springfield (Goodyear) plant, with my parents, was a good looking, Handsome Man. Mrs. Ortiz was tall for her age. She was attractive, I must say, and curvy shaped hips. She was a Cheerful and wanted the best for us. She had a habit of bitting her nails and she smoked. As usual as we were in class there were a few new students. Vincent Robinson was in my class. He failed the 3rd grade and he was with me. Then there was Sean Lane, a very grown kid if I may admit. His father was a big time, popular Quarterback at E.E. Smith High School. He was dark skinned as a street. But he was very muscular kid. He kept himself with a close hair cut with "waves" in his appearance but he loved sports. He could fight and would take on any kid, believe me no matter how big you were. Sean spoke what was on his mind and didn't give a damn either. Then there was Cynthia Horner, a cute little sassy mouth girl just as Ivy Wright and Shenikka McNeil and Janice Wallace who was still with us too.

Third Grade was just a regular class but of course, my behavior was slowly being noticeable. Vincent Robinson and Sean Lane already cliqued. Me, I wanted to be with them. Sean would push me to the side. I looked up to them. Vincent, still didn't care too much for me despite that fight we had a few weeks later. Since he had a high-pitched voice he didn't let nothing stand in his way. "Little Man" had to be tough because he didn't want nobody teasing him. Like I said, he was a very active Kid.

Mrs Ann Ortiz was Ortiz was just a regular teacher. She cared about her job as a teacher. She didn't like the Wild Ricky Holmes. That runt would give Mrs Ortiz a serious hard time. But as for discipline, She was verbally commanding to get class in order. I just dealt with her. Though she knew I was sneaky at times.

Now, we had a new principal, Sr Ellen. She was a short , little, puny petite woman. She played an acoustic guitar. Wearing the same hard rimmed glasses but they were wide glasses just like Sr Saundra. Conducted herself in very proper manner. This Nun was adamant that you would address her as "Yes sister" "No sister". Sr Ellen wanted me out of that school because me being at the "Peace Corner". Her tenure as principal at St Ann School was (1979-1982), That fucker tried her damndest to have me expelled. I think she had a surveillance on me. I'm serious. Every little thing I did I would end up in the "Peace Corner" she would have a look. A scorn expression on her face and look at me. Whenever it came to me, she wouldn't hesitate to take discipline on me. I hated her.

During my time at St Ann School, every Friday morning, the school had to attend church at the Social Hall. Morning mass services. Each student from each grade would be assigned to read a scripture from the Bible. And of course, The nuns playing their acoustic guitars and singing songs, "Day by Day" "Pass it On" and "Sing to the Moutains".

But as my school work it was good. Mrs Ortiz was a exceptional teacher but she wasn't good when it comes to discipline. I knew at times, she was comical when she tried to keep her class in check. But she was always ALWAYS protective of her son.

As students, we really didn't have any fun. We had 2 field trips. I couldn't go to neither of them.

At home, was the Same 'ol. Same'ol. I have to declare that during this period in my life I got the worst Spankings. Any little thing that my Father heard about me of what I did at that Damn school. Daddy would get Hyped up and The Leather Belt would be in his grasp. End of story. As for Sean Lane and Vincent Robinson, they knew my Father. I will repeat, they Knew my Father.

But my Dad was always wondering why Mrs Ortiz was afraid of him. He would say disconcertedly and He Just couldn't sum her up. Maybe, my father's Facial expression was always stern and he had a responsibility. Working at a Tire plant, loving his fragile wife and supporting three Children was his main priority. He was a Man.

I kept my hobby in drawing. Drawing was a way of expressing my enjoyment. Sketching and using Crayola Crayons in my left hand to present my love of the Man from Nazareth. I had dream that I wanted to be a Biblical Artist like Richard and Frances Hook. I just adored their work. With so much enthusiasm, I bought a BIBLE PICTURE Book then I would be in the den looking at illustrations. I would absorb the Christ. The Annunciation. The Nativity. The Ministry. The Passion. THE RESURRECTION and THE ASCENSION. So colorful and rich, it attracted me believing That I could accomplish anything If I put my mind to it. Underrated, The husband and wife artist team would be an integral part of my Childhood.

I have a DEEP, DEEP, DEEP LOVE of Music. No doubt. At home we purchased a new Stereo. A REALIST Record Player with two Speakers. Saturday evenings were a time of enjoying music. Teasie, Tonya or I would turn off our GE TV that had only 3-5 channels. WRAL, WTVD and WECT. We were even getting Channel 28 WKFT that was in Raleigh and Cary, NC. Also, on top of that we would get this Channel in FLORENCE, SOUTH CAROLINA!!

We played our 45 Motown records and many others on that little electronic stereo. Mom and Dad would dance. Performing dances they grew up as teenagers in the late 50's to the time they got married in South Carolina. There was no doubt that my parents were in love with each other.

As of course, I concentrated on my work and I did the best that I can in school. The Kids got along fine. And from time to time, Mrs Ortiz noticed my behavior and always sent me to the "Peace Corner". Sr Ellen, was becoming a Problem for me. You must have her complete attention when corrects you. Like I said, she wanted me out of that school with her phony proper mannerisms.

During this interim, Tonya was having a romantic crush on this musician from Minneapolis, MN. She loved the Family Vocal Group, DeBarge (James was her favorite) and of course the future King of Pop.

KICKBALL was a highly favorite sport among the Kids during recess at school. I'm serious. It was no Joke. It was Fun. Very Fun, indeed. To think about it now, the wide spread field. All kids must pay attention to this game. Certain grades played against each other. But you have to be fair. It was like Dodge Ball. You pitched the Red Ball, like a bowling ball. You kick it and you quickly run for First Base, Second Base, Third Base and Home. But you have to be aware getting hit by the ball from the Boys. There were some Legends. It all depends how far or how high you kick the Ball. There were some great times. Sometimes, the boys get carried away throwing the ball at the Girls hitting them roughly. Majority of the Girls would cry and you have to apologize to them. We have adversaries. My class did. It was with a group of four Friends that still exists to this day. Eddie White (the ringleader), Matthew Bradley (who played and could kick the Ball out of the field into the cemetery. He was short and stocky, played soccer but he had a powerful kick), I have to say he was more mature than out of the four. Tiecel McKoy (chubby and would Gossip like an old Damn woman at church on Sundays. Stupidly grinning. Always talking about somebody) and Kowalski Plummer (with his Big Afro and hyena-like laugh,). They were very athletic in every game they would play during recess. They all looked out for each other. If those any of those four find anything different about you. You would get teased Big time. They were audacious enough to crack on kids who a few grades ahead of them. Especially the girls. They knew their ways and tolerated each other. They defended each other too. Sometimes, they would tease each other. But they always remained loyal to each other and you could say they were Brothers. They were THE FOUR HORSEMEN OF THE APOCALYPSE. But there were others that were part of that clique, A kid named Demond, with a cropped curly Afro and another kid named Bushy.

Sean Lane and Vincent Robinson were not afraid of them at all. When came playing Tag-Football, Basketball on the little black concrete court. As for me, I kept to myself but over my years at that school I would be in conflict with those four.

But Sean and Vincent were fond of Michael Ortiz because he could run so fast. They would choose him over me to play Basketball. It angered me. I guess they didn't give me a chance. All I wanted to do was play.

One thing I hated the most being a student at St Ann's was those reading groups. I hated them. See, you have to be placed in certain reading groups based on your progress, knowledge and reading skills. It was very needless though.

Bazzar- May 1980. I forgot our presentation that Saturday. I think it was a dance but I didn't get to participate in it. I was sporting some white new shoes called NIKE and my somewhat wide-like bell bottomed Jeans. I remember that Teasie and Tonya had to bake a cake or a pie for the festival. There was a Soldier that grilled some good Hamburgers.

As of being in the Third Grade, I was passed to the Fourth Grade. I was glad that I didn't have to deal with Mrs Ann Ortiz. Out of all teachers, there would be one that I would get in the most trouble with. And to this Day, I would never figure out why Sr Ellen hired this Woman to teach the Fourth Grade. Of my unruly Behavior and couldn't practice self control would constantly land me in trouble in the years to follow at that school. I was warned. Oh Yes. I was cautioned. I was just an impressionable kid. Yes, she sensed my behavior. She understand my magnificent fondness for her would cost me my school work, academically. With vexation and extreme disgust, I must say her name was Denise Lugo.

SUMMER — 1980

Summer was like all the others at "THE BOTTOM". My sister Teasie left and enlisted in the US Navy. Tonya, 13 and I just turned,ten, spent that summer having our fun. Tonya went to Georgia with her friend from School, Nicole Smith. My first cousin, Gregory Carter got married. I knew he was a happy man. The night before, there was a huge Cookout at his father's house. Oh, Uncle Mayfield "Chocolate", (my father's Brother-in- law), had food galore. Fried Fish, Fried Chicken, everything that related to Soul Southern Cooking he had it. But I couldn't stay my parents had to take me home. I was getting sleepy. As, for me, I was at the YMCA. The recreational activities I enjoyed was playing the Pin Ball Machine and Foos Ball. I got along with some of the kids there. The counselors were not that bad. But as you know me, I was all over the place. I made friends despite my silliness. Much of the kids lived in Van Story, Haymont, around Fort Bragg road and Raeford road attended the YMCA. They were permanent members. But I wasn't. I was considered a "Drop In". The kids would go on field trips. Camping. Bowling. And Going to CAROWINDS in Charlotte. Carowinds was a Big amusement park in North Carolina. I remembered the radio commercial. "At Carowinds, it's not too far away. At Carowinds". That summer was special because there was a continuation. A sequel to George Lucas' sci-fi epic. STAR WARS EPISODE V: THE EMPIRE STRIKES BACK. Back then the Fans called it "Star Wars II". People, I was in for a treat. Earlier that year, somehow Dad and I went to The Eutaw Theater and we saw the original "Star Wars". We arrived because there was hardly anybody there in theater. It was near the end. The

Battle of Yavin. John Williams' heroic Music at the End of the credits. The Silver Screen was Dark and silent. Suddenly, there was a NEW spectacular trailer to STAR WARS. "Luke Skywalker and Han Solo rescued the Princess. Destroy the Death Star But their story didn't end there!!" All new exciting footage. I will never never forget seeing the Millennium Flacon going through the Asteroid Field as the Tie Fighters chasing it. The Luke Skywalker and Darth Vader lightsaber duel. Han Solo pulling out his laser gun to shoot the Evil Sith Lord. The romance between Han and Princess Leia. All that I saw was snow. I'm telling you, this new movie was coming this summer of 1980. I was so excited. I didn't get the title yet, "The Empire Gets Back" I would murmur to myself. But there was one person that came to my mind: Mark Michel. It was talk of the School that late May, Especially, Derek Sellers was telling me and few others in Class about Luke Skywalker getting stuffed in a Taun-Taun monster, by his friend Han. At home, Tonya said something like Luke gets his hand cut off by Vader. This time, I saw the TV Spots. I was so excited. My father took me to see it at a theater on Village Drive. Our Heroes were meeting their fates. To conclude this, It was nothing like the first time seeing it. It was more of a suspense and dark than the first one.

At the YMCA, I bought trading cards of the Empire Strikes Back with the other kids. Oh, I wished that I could've kept those cards. There was talk about a 12 Film-Cycle, George Lucas' wanted to focus on the Adventures of Luke Skywalker. I know this. An older kid was reading a STARLOG magazine talked about the new projects Lucas' planned to do. I was excited. More Star Wars films coming.

August-1980 – St Ann School – Fourth Grade. Okay, here we go.

$2$2 year old, Puerto-Rican American, from Ohio, Denise Lugo was my 4th grade teacher. She was a beautiful tall, light tanish skin complexioned, oval- shaped face, lovely posed, with an attractive Feminine figure and Long luscious jet-black hair. Recently Graduated from Methodist College (Methodist University). With a Spanish Accent as she spoke English as well as her native language. She loved "Chilli Willie the Penguin "and singer Barry Manilow. The first day of School, all the Boys in Class couldn't get enough of her. I couldn't get take my eyes off of her. We had a new slew of students. Tracy Desert, Danielle Ely (more about her), the bratty Kelly Giles, Genevieve Beateau. Also this ugly girl named Patricia, Teddy Swift and Matthew Vaughan teased a lot. She came later that school year and she went.

My crush on Miss Lugo was immediate. She was the talk of the school as you could well imagine. But this was the symptoms of the Bipolar kicking in. High extremes. Hyper Mania. She gave us cupcakes as treats for us. And she played music on the little green record player. Now, the older Kids knew about her. Tonya was in the 8th grade, her last year. Her teacher was Miss Jacobs. The girls studied Miss Lugo almost immediately. How she conducted and carried herself. Few of them disliked her. We had a new nun that helped us out. A young Brunette named Sister Martha. She was around Miss Lugo's Age and was recently a nun. She gave up all her fun life and her motorcycle to God Almighty. Yes, She played the

55

acoustic guitar too. Sr Martha was okay. She was friendly. I never really had any issues with her. She taught Physical Education. She socialized with all the Kids.

I was really certain that I would do well academically in class with Miss Lugo. I went through extreme moods. The Moody rollercoaster was in effect. Little did I know that my grades would slip tremendously. I had lack of interest of doing my work. The kids in my class already knew about my clownish and silly behavior.

Miss Lugo already aware that I had a hard stern Father. She used that against me. Also, that preposterous Sr Ellen. Sean Lane and Vincent Robinson sensed that she was trouble. But the issue was that she didn't conduct herself as a mannered School teacher. How she dressed. When it came to discipline, she was unfair. Only to the Boys, She was not fair at all. Like Sister Janice, I was her puppet. Sr Ellen, Sr Saundra and Mrs Smith would always protected Miss Lugo when it came to me of course. Don't bother Miss Lugo. So whenever Miss Lugo would call my Dad or have Tonya bring Dad. Sr Ellen and Miss Lugo had me in a world of Shit. But the point was she couldn't control her class. Dad would say, "I let the Belt do the talking". She did appreciate my love for Biblical art. Yet, She was constantly on me. Sending me to the "Peace Corner".

Michelle "Call Her Misty" Balsamo was highly Fond of Miss Lugo. To this day, if you ask Michelle who was her favorite teacher she would answer immediately, "Miss Lugo". Danielle Ely and Juliet Smith liked her too.

YES! YES! The crush was still there. I strongly believed that whenever Miss Lugo would leave school after doing grading her papers. She would go home. She would talk to her mother in Spanish about me. Again, I was always getting into trouble when it came to her. My Father couldn't understand it. This was about the time, he was thinking about taking me out of St Ann's. But such was not the case.

Then Indian summer came. One day in October in class, Miss Lugo received word that her mother was sick and physically ill. I remember that day. She had to leave immediately. It was urgent. I remember the sad and anxious expression on her face. Tears were in her eyes. She was absent for a few days. We as kids, felt sympathetic towards her. So, we decided make some get well cards for her Family. I wanted to do my best to make the best "Get Well" Card for her. So at the end of the day afternoon, Mike Ortiz and I told his mother as she was leaving. She said that was a Good thing for us to do. We wanted to let her know that we care for Miss Lugo and her Family during that troubling time.

September 1980 – The NBC mini-series SHOGUN premiered starring Richard Chamberlin. I didn't really understood it. My Dad and Tonya watched the series. An entertaining Epic story. "Another one Bites to Dust" was the Big Song by the Rock Group, Queen. Sean, Vincent and Teddy would use that song against THE FOUR HORSEMEN OF THE APOCALYPSE when we played Kick Ball against them.

December 1980

Miss Lugo was at the point of not taking any chances on me. Me "Cutting up" in Class. I didn't see it. Yes, I talked excessively loud and making a clown of myself. My Grades were not good at all. Then one day, it either Sr Ellen or Miss Lugo called my Father. Sean Lane and I had to stay after class for a one hour detention. That was what Miss Lugo and Sr Ellen wanted to do. Bad Behavior Correction Procedure. That Friday Afternoon, I was cleaning the blackboard. My Father was already there at the Principal's Office and Miss Lugo was present, with her arms folded having a spiteful expression on her face. Dad had just came home from work. As my father wanted to point out that there was someone calling "racist" names. They didn't care about that. So, I returned to the Classroom and got my book bag. Sean Lane (with his grown self), asked me plainly, "You gonna get a whoopin?" I nodded yes.

In truth, I was having a slow absorbing and rising hatred for her. Though I was still having outlandish crush that blinded me terribly. It also during this time, I was rambling and talking to myself when I was holding something inside me. I couldn't express myself. I just remained quiet.

Saturday, December 13, 1980.

Miss Lugo organized a party at her house. The cause was that her class sent her mother those nice "Get Well" cards. Rightly so, she got well. It was a sunny day. The plan was to meet Miss Lugo at the school so she could follow her to her house. She lived off McArthur Road and between Rosehill Road. In truth, My Father didn't want to take me. But he went along with the program. Mike Ortiz pissed me off by telling me to "Shut up" because I said something. That Incensed me. We had participated "Kris Kringle" and all the kids exchanged Gifts to each other. I got a gift from Danielle Ely and it was a truck, I remember. Forrest Alvarez, being a Clown was Crazy about Miss Lugo. But never disciplined him or his twin sister April. Her house was very nice and oriented. The living room was highly decorated. Nice couches. And there was a picture of Miss Lugo and her eldest Sister Patricia as little girls wearing white cap and gowns like they were graduating from school. Highly Manic and overly excited, I couldn't stay still. I knew that Vincent Robinson didn't want to be around me that day. Two of the great things that happened that day. One was Miss Lugo's two pet chihuahuas, "Bono and Queenie". She loved those dogs even Sean wanted to see them because he jokingly talked about them in class. We saw them. I think that Queenie was Blind out of the two. Tempermental small dogs that barked constantly. Then the Big suprise came for us was her mother came to their den. In return of all those get well cards all of her class had made. We were given the 1981 McDonald's Coloring Calendar. After that, we met her Uncle Joe, nice kind man. He heard alot about me. I wasn't suprised though. So, the rest of that day was spent us hanging out in her backyard. Despite of the poop from Bono and Queenie. It wasn't all over the yard. No. Just a little bit of it. The day ended and the party was over and my father picked me up to take me home.

The Christmas Holidays came. Tonya and I had a good Christmas. I got some Star Wars toys. A snow speeder, a red plastic light-saber, MERLIN and the SIMON game from Parker-Brothers. And our relatives came by to visit us.

A new decade began. The EIGHTIES. A lot was going in my life and the world. New Wave music and Punk Rock was emerging. A new toy that became an immediate fad, The Rubik's Cube. The catch phrase was, "Where's the Beef?" yelled an ansty elderly lady from a commercial by Wendy's Hamburgers. It was the Reagan Years. Our beloved Beatle, John Lennon was violently taken away from us. A terrible Space shuttle exploded with seven crew members shocked the World as we looked on. The NFL Football team was the San Francisco 49ers. Wearing stylish Jeans was the main fashion among the youth. Later that decade, a deadly disease that was an epidemic and struck the Gay community. Our ignorance and prejudice caused a reason for people to utter, "It's God's punishment for gay men" I must admit, we were wrong. The disease also caused a crisis to the women and children. It became a disease that effected us all and the world.

The New Year. 1981. It was the same old song. Now this time, Sean, Vincent and I had to deal with THE HORSEMEN OF THE APOCALYPSE. Playing Kick Ball was serious stuff. We knew we had to deal with Matt Bradley's outstanding kick of the Ball. Our Kickball field had us stationed to certain locations. I was positioned at left. April Alvarez, liked to play too. She would Be on First base. Vincent and Sean was spread out farther. The playground only had those hard piped monkey Bars. Climbing bars and a Slider.

My Grades were in serious jeopardy. At home, I was more worries about getting the spankings Big Time. My mother would get my Father all hyped up. Instigated it. I already had built up rage in me.

Now, this is the lesson at 734 Eufaula Street. You do what Dad and Mom instruct you to do. No ifs, ands, buts about it. My father wouldn't hesitate to grab me. I had no one to talk to. With my behavioral issues at school combined with my hassles with my parents, I felt that I was trapped. But talking to myself was my way out.

SPRING. EASTER. – APRIL, 1981

Report Card Day. My Mother and I arrived at school. Miss Lugo showed it to us and explained the reason her giving me my grades. Oh, I felt down. That day, my mother highly upset. Since it was Tonya's last year at St Ann's, her grades were very good. But I think it was Math that she struggled. "Travis didn't do a thing in school!" said my Mother with great disappointment. My only worry was you know who.

Returning to school, I was very disappointed. No one realized it but I was. Sean Lane, Teddy Swift and Derek Sellers were suspended by Miss Lugo during that time. Senseless Bullshit. And I was next, even Miss Lugo told me, "Travis, You're on thin ice."

May 1981– Bazzar. I ate like a Hog there. Eating a Big Cake. I must say, I adored Food. Eating all Junk Food. Never ate any Salads. I had a Big Appetite. Seriously. All my classmates knew it. Tonya was wondering what's wrong with him? I have a Story to share with you later.

Field Day was a traditional Olympics event. Usually, Held in late May. All the Classes participated. There were competitions of sorts. But there was one I received 2nd ribbon for the soft ball Throw. Also, KickBall was the game to play as well.

June-1981

As I struggled through the Fourth Grade, I passed to the Fifth Grade. BARELY. Of course as you know I was Hyper Manic As Hell. I was a fool enough to tell Mrs Ortiz that I passed. I don't why I told her. Earlier, That day, I was just like Daffy Duck because in the Beginning of the School Miss Lugo wanted our Birthdates. Somehow, she got my Birthdate wrong, I gave her my father's Birthdate though I gave her mine. Sean and few of the kids laughed and that's what made me upset. I was loud and I told Miss Lugo that looked at me. "You're embarrassed". She got direct on me.

"What did you say to me?", Miss Lugo asked me being upset. She didn't like to be corrected. NO. NO. NO.

"You're embarrassed, I told you my Birthdate was June 16ᵗʰ. I was just out of control. Getting upset. I was afraid that she would send me to the "Peace Corner". Now, I had this habit of kissing Miss Lugo. I did. Did it all the time. She was my "Dream Girl". So, to calm me down she gave me a present; a 45-record "Your Kiss is on My List" by Daryl Hall and John Oates. Big Hit on the Top 10 Billboard Music Chart, that late Spring. Sean and Mike would sing the chorus. I felt better after being ridiculed in class.

THE LAST DAY OF SCHOOL.

Miss Lugo planned a trip for us. The Roller Skating Rink at Boone Trail/Village Drive. We had our fun. I knew how to skate when I was at the YMCA. We didn't have to wear our uniforms. But there was an accident. Genevieve Beateau hit her forehead against the wall on the skating floor. Poor Genevieve was crying as we saw Miss Lugo's sister Patricia took her to the Hospital. It was just an accident. When we got back to class. We acted like a bunch antics from Looney Tunes. Members of Miss Lugo's Family were at her class. Yes, I passed to the Fifth Grade But I strongly believed Miss Lugo was concerned about me going to the Fifth Grade. To admit this now, I wasn't ready.

My sister Tonya graduated From St Ann School also that June.

Back at THE BOTTOM. I wanted to play Baseball at LAMON STREET PARK. The Pirates. We wore Yellow and White uniforms. Debbie Douglas, Carla's second eldest sister knew Tootsie, a cool laid back Brother from the neighborhood, CAMPBELL TERRACE. I went to practice there at the Baseball field. He didn't think I was good enough. I was on the team anyway that summer. There were tough areas in Fayetteville which the Population was African-American. GROVE VIEW TERRACE, CAMPBELL TERRACE (as I mentioned earlier), BLUEBERRY, MOUNT SIANAI, SAVOY HEIGHTS (Sivi Collins lived there), EVANS HILL, NORTH STREET and THE BOTTOM. Carla was very good playing baseball. I played only one Game. Most of that summer, I sat on the Bench. But there was one Kid who knew that I had potential, Darren. He knew that I had an ARM. I could throw a Baseball.

I got injured at the Park. I didn't know what happened to me that evening. My father and Tootsie helped me up from the ground. I was knocked unconsciously by a tire swing hooked by a chain. The kids on the team witnessed it. It was a hot day that June. Suddenly, I woke up in my bed the next morning. That summer, My Father took me to see SUPERMAN II. A good Film. The last survivor of Krypton battles 3 evil nemesis from his destroyed home planet on Earth. He would Fall in Love with Lois Lane. And he wanted to be with her and his powers were taken away because of his love for her. And he pays an ultimate price. What can Superman do? Superman regains his powers. Battle the Kryptonian criminals and save the day for his new home planet, Earth. Tonya stayed up late to watch the "Wedding of the Century", Prince Charles and Lady Diana. Later that year, in November, my father took Tonya and I to see another great film about an adventurous Archeologist. In my own world, in our backyard, I wanted to be like that iconic hero. Sometimes, I play by myself. Rambling to myself and I ordered a comic Book at School, I was so excited to read it. Actor, Harrison Ford was one of my few heroes and he was everywhere in Hollywood Cinema.

Extra Credit: We had a Family Dog. Pooh-Bear, A Pekingese. (May 1981-Nov 1986). Cute Dog. My cousin, Greg Carter and he had one too, named Ivy. He was emotionally attached to Tonya. He was rough towards me because I was picking on him. He constantly Barked at me. He was alright. But Our big mistake with him was we fed him too much. Human food. We didn't know at that time. He didn't like Dog Food at all. Very defensive. Hair was all over the house furniture and Mom didn't like that. But towards the end it was the Fleas that give him a Hard time. He developed a Skin Disorder. Unfortunately, We had to give him up. Tonya was sad for a long time because when she started attending College, NCSU. She never saw her dog again.

August- 1981.

5th Grade. We had new Students added to the Bunch. Most of them, Military Brats: Charlotte Hales, Lori Hoskins, Jennifer Rathke and John Senninger. Chris Anderson (a Real Creep), I met him at the YMCA that summer. He was Forrest Alvarez's greatest adversary. Derek never liked him either.

Mrs. Betsy Rafferty was our teacher. A native of New Hampshire. Her husband was in the Military. The Air Force and She had 2 Children. A son (my Age) and a daughter. This Woman was a Character. She was a very voluptuous, curvy shaped. A Brunette. She had very Thick Dark Brown Hair that was almost Black. It was styled like Feathered Princess Diana very much so. She had pale white skin. No color. She had a gap in her teeth. She strongly resembled actress, Adrienne Barbeau. Very Sarcastic with a voice like Lavern from the comedy hit Show, "Lavern and Shirley". She had a Northern Sassy accent. She was attractive, I must say. She always dressed professionally. But she had this Flirty Girlish disposition about herself. Looking Back, She was probably Boy-Crazy as if she was a dancer in a burlesque show. She was crazy about hunk actor Tom Selleck. And a loyal Boston Celtics Fan.

I really had some serious issues with her as I will explain. Like Miss Lugo, I don't know what in the Hell or Why in the Hell Sr Ellen hired her. She was a tough teacher I must admit. I'm not going to say she's an exceptional teacher. NO. But I just couldn't keep up with her. The thing that really pissed me off about her was that she always mistaken me for Derek Sellers. Derek and I do not look like each other. She would call me "Derek". But the problem with Mrs

Rafferty and I was that we just didn't get along at all. And Yes, I was constantly in trouble with her. The Presence of Sr Ellen was lurking around.

School began as usual. Yes, I missed Ms Lugo. But THE FOUR HORSEMEN OF THE APOCALYPSE, now had to deal with her.

I was trying to do my best academically. I felt that I was in a boxing match with Mrs Rafferty. And she was just jabbing and punching. She had me against the ropes. And those Damn Reading groups. She always sarcastic and putting us down. I didn't like that. Hell, we were just Kids.

We had fun from time to time. Mrs Rafferty noticed my behavior, of course. But there one kid that really touched me. A girl. She spoked up for me. Much to my suprise. She was vocal from time to time. Just turned eleven. A military Brat, like most of the kids in my class. I really liked this girl. Honestly, from time to time, I thought about her.

At home, life was the same thing. Dad would grab me in a minute. But there were concerns about my mother's Behavior that caught our attention, Especially Tonya. I remember Tonya later admitting that mom went to the Doctor's office. Dr Vick, I believe. According to her, He told my Father that she had a chemical imbalance in her brain. We didn't know what a chemical imbalance was but we will for sure and we will see it in several years.

During this time, I was establishing and forming Friendships with the kids at school. Derek Sellers and Forrest Alvarez, of course. Derek was the kind of kid that would spoil everything about the movies his Father took him to go see. Derek was "pickified" and he was a prankster. But he would have his temper tantrums. His mother was a Good looking Woman. WHOOO! She was attractive. He would always tell jokes and making funny sounds. To be honest with you, I never really had any issues with Ivy Wright's first cousin. He made me laugh. But I must say he was very loyal as a friend. Forrest was more of a Doctor. His little giggling and proper Linus Van Pelt mannerism talk amused me. He could be a referee on certain things involving us kids and he had leadership qualities. I was an Altar Boy and Forrest trained me and I learned it quick. With the mean and grumpy Fr Roache during 7:00pm Mass on Saturday Evenings, He was just a grumpy old man. Well, we had to tolerate the big Flounder. Though. Forrest was sneaky and understanding as a boy of eleven. I know to this day, if we ever meet, we would pick up right where we left off.

I had this love for singing and the teacher and my classmates. The First to notice that was Sr Janice (UGH!). Miss Lugo, Sr Ellen, my Fifth Grade teacher and Mrs Birdell Smith. I didn't know that next special talent that I inherited from in my family but I just loved singing.

Along with the nuns a new one was added to the bunch. Sr Mary Phyllis. A very supportive and funny. A Tall Heavy set Women with her thick glasses. I think she was more of a helper for the teacher's students who have difficulty keeping up with the class. A den mother. She would tickle the Hell out of when it came to discipline when she gets upset with her very low Bossy Talk. But she could be nice and understanding. I never had any real issues with her.

As the days passed, Came Autumn. Mrs Rafferty made us perform a Play for some of the Classes. THE LEGEND OF SLEEPY HOLLOW by author Washington Irving. We had to memorize our lines and we practised a week. Sean Lane was chosen to play Ichabod Crane. Misty Balsamo was the Narrator. I played the Telegraph Man. It was a short play. Mrs Rafferty's Husband came and brought some tools to create the stage play. A Tall Man with front Buck Teeth. Neatly cut and trimmed short hair. He was wearing his Uniform. Just a short sleeve shirt and blue khaki pants with his name tag. He had an electric Screwdriver and he drilled a hole on both side of the wall in our room and he used a metal hook to keep the wire line. He screwed it there. Since the setting of the story was in the 1700's, Mrs Rafferty created that period. For the Boys, we wore long sleeve shirts and we had to make our hats out of Black construction paper, I Think. We had to pull our blue pants to our ankle length. The Girls were made to wear gowns. It was pretty good for us to do that. But I wanted to play Ichabod Crane. I was so shocked to learn that there was a Sleepy Hollow in New York.

The report cards came out in late October 1981. My grades suffered. Dad, of course was upset. He didn't even talked to Tonya and I. Now, when it came to School work. Dad put an emphasis on Education. She said wait until Dad gets home. Dad didn't talk to us on that Friday evening. Tonya was a 9$^{th\ grade}$ student at St Patrick School on Fort Bragg Road. I don't think she liked it. But the School was large enough to have the Nuns who were the Daughters of Emmitsburg, MD, Lived there. Yes, they all lived there at a much Big Brick Building with a nice yard behind the School with a small fence surrounding it. But I'll remembered it was quiet as a Catholic Church over there.

Mrs Rafferty, I must be honest. She did try to encourage me to improve my school work. When my mother came to pick me up and I was in Miss Lugo class after school as I always do. Mrs Rafferty was there and they spoke. Mom asked her how I was doing in class. Mrs Rafferty replied blunty, in her Northern accent, "Careless. Careless". It was Sr Mary Phyllis to the rescue as she tried to help me and work with me on my Reading and Math. But it didn't seem to go through to me. I was trying believe me. I was really trying.

Our class went to Field trips. But as the same time I was constantly in school trouble with Lavern. One time, Mrs Rafferty made write a Report on a Dictionary all day in class. My Hatred towards her was already evident. GRRRR!!

Christmas Holidays Came. Our Music Teacher, Mrs Holt taught us music and she would play her piano and we had to perform a song for a Christmas musical Play at the Social Hall. "Do you Hear what I hear?" I noticed my voice was very loud. Sean Lane and a few others knew it too. Like I said, I loved Singing. The name of the Play was TOYLAND, performed by Miss Lugo's class. It was dark because there was a light focusing on us. A Spotlight. Some of the kids forgot their lines wrong but it was fun. Enjoyable. All the Kids did their best. Childhood innocence.

As the Christmas Break was near. The last day before the break, We were supposed to have a Christmas Party. Since my Class was different. We were all rowdy. Mrs Rafferty warned us if we keep misbehaving badly there would be NO CHRISTMAS PARTY! Now, How in the Hell as us Kids, could understood that warning?? We tried. But there was one student that kept on talking in Class. We just had to be quiet for a week or so. Kelly Giles. And then, the Party was off. Nothing. We didn't have a Party like the rest of the school. We were so angry at Kelly and she would say, "It's not my fault". Kelly Giles was a cute girl with a pouty expression with a Blonde Wedge Dorothy Hamill Hairstyle. Most of the Girls had that style. Especially, Maggie Burns. Kelly spoke her mind. Mike Ortiz and Matt Vaughn had crushes on her. But I think it was Michael she was head over heels for. Or Both of them. She tried her damndest to get me in trouble. Unfortunately, No party for us.

Christmas 1981 was very Special for us. Teasie came home from California, wearing this Curl. Her hair was short and looking pretty with this new Hairstyle. It was called the California Curl among African-Americans. Michael Jackson and all entertainers was sporting it. My mother also with her sisters had that "Jerri Curl" with the curl Gel conditioner to keep it nice, Bright and Shiny. Men sported the "Jerri Curl" too. I never liked it. We had a Big Dinner held at our house. My mother's relatives and cousins came. Mom cooked Christmas Dinner with Teasie and Tonya helping her in the kitchen. Dad's older Brother came, "Uncle D" and his son Terry. There was Food Galore and it was in our little Dining room. Grab a plate and help yourself.

After the Holidays, Classes resumed at St Ann. Late January 1982, The report cards came. My report Card and the grades were not good at all. At home, Dad was furious. Arguing, in disbelief, He didn't even talk to me for a week or so. Damn. My parents couldn't understand what was going on. My head held down as I sat down our den couch. Feeling sad...and eventually I wept.

What I got for Christmas was a mini small tape recorder with a radio from one speaker. From Radio Shack, I believe. I loved it so much. I was sneaky and record my family talk or myself singing and I would take the paper holder off the wire clothes hanger. Use two of them as drum sticks and I would beat on books and couch pillows.

Going at it and making beats off my head. It would annoy Dad to the highest around the house. Outside in our back yard, I would get two wooden sticks and get our gray plastic trash can and I would go at it.

Well, at school we had a new physical education teacher. He was military. Big, burly with a military crew cut. He loved UNC Basketball. He had an awkward walk and Sean Lane and Vincent Robinson would mock his walk. Eventually, he would become a teacher at our school. Mr Toht.

During this time, I was having some serious, serious with Mrs Rafferty. I didn't want to deal this woman. Tensions grew between us. The GODDAMN Sr Ellen was on the alert to call my parents to have me suspended or expelled. I knew this incident was on a Friday morning in Reading Class, I was talking back to Mrs Rafferty. And she sends me to the "Peace Corner". So, as I walked out of class, Mrs Rafferty tried to grab my arm and I jerked it away. Sr Ellen was ready and She would give me these looks to discipline me. And our new Secretary, Mrs Chaffin, would sometimes give me looks and shake her head. Always Me. I was there in the "Peace Corner". It was a like a second home for me. I remember one time, Trina Collins would do the "Shame on you" expression on her fingers when she saw me as she walked down the Hall. Sr Ellen had a talk with me. I was called back to class. I was so furious I just didn't want to talk. I returned class and sat down, with my arms folded. Not saying a word. Mrs Rafferty asked me gently if I could behave and be with the class. It was Math class. I didn't answer. Mrs Rafferty exploded out of her chair in desk and told me to go back to the "Peace Corner" and I got up and returned. At first, I turned around and said that I was sorry but Mrs Rafferty wouldn't have nothing of it. She pointed her finger and directed me out. I was back in the "Peace Corner". Again. Sr Ellen, looking that this was it. So, Sr Ellen made Mrs Rafferty go this little Special conference Room with a table a two chairs but we were standing. There was Sr Ellen, Mrs Rafferty and I. Their eyes all studied on me. Sr Ellen asked me why I didn't apologize to her. I made up some lie saying that, "I was afraid". They all looked at me with such Scorn and contempt. Mrs Rafferty, that what she wanted from me. An apology. I returned to class. End of story.

As I was being "The Problem Child" at School. I was enjoying listening to music to my little tape recorder. Fayetteville had a new radio station for the African-American youth. D-103 FM. It was beating out WIDU and WFLB. It played all the hip tunes during that time and I enjoyed listening to D-103 FM.

Bazzar- May 1982, I think at this one I was the life of the Party. I participated in games and I won a few big bottles of Mountain Dew. Danielle Ely was very encouraging. I had a little crush on her. Mrs Rafferty came and she looked at more of the Arts and Craft on display in the Social Hall. Then all of a sudden, A kid that was in My previous class, came to the event with his mother. Teddy Swift. But I saw a different side of him. He was more mature. He enjoyed the new school he was attending. As we talked I told him that I didn't like my teacher, "She really sucks". Teddy Laughed as we both walked through at the center of the festival. In some ways, I was proud that he was doing well at another school. That was the last time I ever saw him.

Spring came. Our music teacher, Mrs Holt planned a musical play for us. 5th- 8th grade. LIGHTSHINE! It was a musical that emphasized on the Beatitudes of Christ on his Sermon on the Mount. The Musical by Buryl Red and Lyrics were by Grace Hawthorne. The play was directed by the speech impediment Mrs Smith and the sarcastic Mrs Rafferty. The students such as Maggie Burns, Michelle Balsamo, the Eanes kids were the actors. Mrs Holt wanted the musical to be the best. But the focal point was this gentle song from the musical called, "Would You". There were tryouts and auditions. I remember in Music Class, I had to sing the lyrics from a small pamphlet. Somehow, I was chosen to sing it. Sense, My "Hyper Manic" self, Mrs Holt was hard on me. Of course, All the Kids had to sing other songs from the play. Now that song was a whole song was sung by a soloist. So Mrs Holt chose me to sing the First Verse and the second verse would be sung by a girl named Stacy. Mrs Holt made us practise and give us tips on how we should present ourselves on our little stage in the Social Hall. Just be natural and sing the song. On that nice spring evening, in May, Our parents were proud. We were all dressed in our best attire. I wore a light brown suit, with a yellow shirt, with a brown clip on tie and shiny Black shoes. Lori Hoskins complimented on how I look. "You look nice in your suit, Travis." She said proudly. But Vincent Robinson was the best dressed in our class. He wore a White Sports Coat, A Navy Blue tie, Nice Blue pants and a nice Black shoes. "You look Sharp." Said Mrs Rafferty as he strutted in the class as we cheered him on. All the Kids were in the play nervous. But, we gave our all. When it came to for me to sing that gentle song. Mrs Holt and her musicians with Sr Ellen and Sr Martha played their acoustic guitars softly. I started singing softly to the First Verse and I walked as I sung as my voice was getting stronger. Stacy, kept a steady pace as she sung the second Verse and the few of cast members and students came on stage finished the song. After that came a Thunderous Applause from the Audience. Full of anxiety, I came down from stage with tears in my eyes, I thought I messed up. I didn't. It was just like an Exhale. I don't know why I felt that way but my classmates were wondering what was wrong with me. I did my best. I sung "Would You" to the best of my ability as well as Stacy. Now at the end of the Musical, As we left in a straight line. Then all of a sudden, Mrs Ortiz was in the audience with her husband, She saw me and shouted with both her thumbs up. "THAT WAS GREAT TRAVIS!!". So, at the end, there were refreshments served. Mrs Holt was so proud of Stacy and I. She was very Happy.

Though, I still had issues with Mrs Betsy Rafferty. She was getting to move with her Family since she was a military Wife. In Mid-May, Jennifer Rathke's mother planned a going away Party for her. I really didn't care. My main issue with Mrs Rafferty was she was teaching us Religion earlier in the spring about Racism that I didn't agree with. I would blurt out my opinion about Racism and I don't think that woman knew what she talking about or doing. She was doing some exercise like, The "Jane Elliot" Project in Class. Having the Blondes and Brown hair. She tried to separate Blacks and Whites in our class. It didn't work at all. Sean, Vincent, Derek and I would get in more trouble than anybody. I heard stories about her from the other kids. Like, I said earlier, this woman is from New Hampshire and she's White. And there was a large Caucasian-American population at that state to this day. And there's hardly any African-Americans there. I don't think she saw Black people for that matter until she traveled to the South. I might be wrong. As sarcastic as she was she would prattle about how bad we were as a class. Yes, My mouth would get me in trouble. I know that she was trying to help me with my school work. Still, I detested her.

So, as the going away party for Mrs Rafferty was already planned. It was held at the library next to the Kitchen. We all said "SUPRISE!" Few of the teachers gave her cards. She got emotional and started crying. I didn't give a shit. As the party continued with refreshments, there was green sherbert punch and I remember Derek drinking it and he liked it. Somehow, I blurted out a comment about Racism. Mrs Rafferty heard it. So, after party, she told Sr Ellen. I was talking to Danielle Ely and Michelle Balsamo outside in the playground. Sr Ellen approached me and I walked with her to the little conference room. Sr Ellen cautioned me about what I said. As I said earlier, She wanted me expelled. And then I was offended and angry to be exact. I returned to class. Mrs Rafferty was thanking us for the Party. She and her Family was going to Japan.

So, after class was over and all the students left. Mrs Rafferty wanted to talk to me. And wanted to know what Sr Ellen told me and I told her about I didn't like she was doing. I wanted to tell her that I hated her and she was a racist. But, I kept it to myself. Actually, she didn't deserve to have that party by the way she treated us. Nothing was resolved. I left the classroom and I never saw her again.

The last several weeks, Sr Mary Phyllis substituted for Mrs Rafferty. I don't think no one in my class missed her when she left. We never spoke about her really or even mentioned her. Most, of that time, I was getting myself in trouble over stupid shit and Sr Ellen was watching me. I was so glad that that year 1982 was her last year as our School principal.

Of course, the school gave her a farewell party in the Social

Hall, We all said our goodbyes to her. When she looked at me for the last time. It was like, I couldn't describe it. She looked at me with her phony snobby smile. I felt Sheri was being ridiculous. Crying. Sr Ellen left and I guess she was pleased that she didn't have to deal with me anymore.

Last day of School – June 1982. We were given our report cards.... I failed the Fifth Grade. Miserably. There was a letter in it by Mrs Rafferty saying that I needed to take Math, Science, Social Studies and American History over again. I was forced to attend Summer School at Edgewood Middle School.

My Hatred for that Woman was very very passionate. I was talking to myself in my room of what I should have said or done to her when we last talked. But most of all, I was hurt and angry that she failed me. Yes, I must admit I called her on the phone a few times and when she answered I hung up.

IT WASN'T OVER YET.

I attended Edgewood Middle School (now Luther Nicks Jeralds Middle School), (June-August 1982). My mother was adamant that I was going. She and my Father argued about that. As you may know, that summer of '82 was different for me. I had alot of work to do believe me. Homework everyday. The teachers were tough. The Kids were different as I expected. Being disrespectful to the teachers. I remembered one or two teachers, Mrs Hildebrand, a soft, kind lady and another teacher who taught Social Studies, He attended St Ann's Church. But there was one person in my class that had to attend summer school as I. Sean Lane. He looked upset himself being in school for the partial summer and I couldn't blame him. He hardly talked to me. He was in my Social Studies Class. I had to deal with some kids who tried to bully me. One ugly kid from Grove View Terrace or Campbell Terrace, He played Little League Baseball at Lamon Street Park. The Blue and White, Braves was picking a fight with me. But I fought back. And after that he left me alone.

Also, the Boys asked me what was it like going to a "different school". As I waited for my mother to pick me up. Those kids were way out of my league. They were beginning to ask me about sex. As I was teased, bringing up a "Woman's Body". I couldn't even answer their questions. I do recall one kid saying that I was going to be a "Homosexual". I was quiet and I spoke very softly. I was confused. I didn't understand what was going on. Or what those Boys were talking about.

Mom had to drop me off every morning and pick me up and I had to carry those heavy books. I just hated it. And Damn it, Dad had to lecture me about school and getting an education. I was just feeling distressed and angry.

Those last two weeks in August went by fast. I went to the movies. And I saw "ROCKY III". Rocky Balboa, now being a famous boxing champion after defeating Apollo Creed. He was everywhere. Then this Big young Brutish Fighter who challenged Balboa. He had a Gritty Mean look and his Voice is the most recognized voice in all the '80's pop culture. He told the truth about Rocky fighting "Dem, set ups!" As Rocky was announcing his retirement from boxing. His trainer Mickey, didn't want him to fight this young, "Clubber Lang" because he knew he was going to lose this fight. Clubber Lang really tested Rocky by trying to "holler" at Adrian. Rocky was enraged and it was on. The Boxing match was on. Poor Rocky got beaten terribly. Mickey died of a heart attack. Rocky was approached by his former opponent, Apollo Creed. Coaches him to back into the ring. Apollo told him that he has, "The Eye of the Tiger". So, Rocky wanted to do it but he couldn't over Mickey which frustrates Apollo as he was training him. But Adrian and Rocky had it out. Arguing on the Beach, He finally admitted to his wife, "He was afraid". Afraid of losing Mickey. But Adrian and Apollo believes that he could do it. Rocky gets to it and he defeats Clubber Lang. End of Story. I think that actor-director Sylvester Stallone should have ended with this film but he continued the "Italian Stallion Saga".

But it was "Mr T" that I really got a kick out of. His talking was imitated by everyone during that time. An action packed NBC TV show. "The A-Team" was a popular show of the 80's. I must agree that "Mr T" was "The A-Team".

After I finished Summer School, I had the month of August to relax. Though, the presence of Mrs Rafferty wasn't over yet.

*(August 1982-June 1985) were my later years at St Ann Catholic School. My pubescent years. And my body was changing leisurely. This was perhaps the most important period in my life because the symptoms of my Bipolar Type I, was becoming more and more noticeable. And I had to deal with Mrs. Birdell Smith and Miss Lugo Back to Back.

The week of Orientation – August 1982, my mother went to Roses' to purchase notebooks and pencils for me to get ready for school. I was nervous at first because for a Damn short summer going to take Classes during those months (June-July) was difficult. I walked to my School. It wasn't a long walk But i had to be careful crossing the street with light blue IZOD shirt and corduroy pants. I remember when I went to the entrance the 6th Grade Class was the last room to my right down the hall. There was a list posted on the wall the names of the students of 6th Grade. I was nervous to try to find my name of the list. BOOM! There, I was. Much to my suprise, Misty Balsamo was in the hall and we both chatted for a bit. I noticed a change in her. She was more laid back and mature. Misty was never silly, of course. But she was not the "Tattle Tell" girl anymore. Girls always mature much faster than Boys. Misty was the same little saintly girl that reached out to me that first day of school when we were in the first grade. Still, She reached out to me. Mrs Birdell Smith, was in the class talking to the parents of students. She was an average built woman, Light skinned complexioned with an Afro-like styled hair. With a hump back She had some kind of speech impediment as she talked. From Wilmington NC, Her daughters, Michelle (who already graduated from St Ann's the previous year with my sister Tonya and her sister annoying Katina was now attending there). I also saw Derek Sellers much to my suprise and we talked as we walked to the playground. This officially established our friendship. The two of us. That was when I saw his attractive mother ready to pick him up. Now, as I was leaving, Kelly Giles and Mike Ortiz were on those monkey bars. Steel metal pipes. I don't know how us as kids dealt with those hard steel bars but we did.

Sr Saundra was now the Principal at St Ann School and running things. As I walked back home and Kelly and Mike were still talking they both said, "Bye Travis". We waved towards each other. I walked home and I was just thinking. Probably, if I was going to perform well in school this time.

I returned home and went to my room and played my cassette tapes on little tape recorder that I recorded on radio and SUPERMAN: THE

MOVIE that had officially premiered on ABC that early February. That motivated me. Mom took me back to school and she talked to Mrs Smith on what I need to do. She already told her that we went to purchase the notebooks and pencils. Mrs Smith said that was fine.

First day of School in August. I attended school and getting back to the swing of things. And we had new students. Vincent Robinson returned and Sean Lane didn't. I guess this started our friendship but it was awkward and difficult as the years passed. I guess with Sean's absence Vincent had no choice but to stick with me. He noticed my manic behavior as all my classmates did. I strongly felt he just tolerated me. During that day, I saw a light skinned black girl with brown hair. She wore this white IZOD typed skirt with little red rose polka dots designed. She wore green socks and dark red penny loafers. She was attentive in class. She had a skin disorder, of Poison Ivy, she explained to me. But she didn't let that stand in her way or hold her back. She was strong. And I admired her for that. I saw her and I couldn't keep my eyes off of her. I didn't stare at her all day, Alright. Her name was Angela Butler. Then there was Shannon Davis. Shannon was a jubilant girl who liked to have fun. She would take chances. I guess she was enjoying life as it was at the time. Though she made a huge impact on us for attending St Ann School for just one year. Anne (Woody Woopecker), Alex Ewing. She was an all day girl. She loved watching films. A mature girl who joked from time to time. She and I really got along. Allyson Robison, was an introverted girl. I think she was going through some issues. Then, Lorena Shepard returned to St Ann School after a three year absence. Then there was this other young kid who sat across the classroom, who looked like he was lost. He was staring everywhere around the class. But I must say we struck up a friendship immediately that ended in betrayal, His name was Maurice Thomas. He was a skinny kid that was about to turn 11. With a gaunt facial structure with a more of an egged shaped head. As, I must be honest about him was that he was the kind of kid that will figure you out. Just by studying you. There was another student, a heavy set girl with white Blondish hair, I forgot her name. Then, Finally there was another kid I have to say we tolerated him because of a Health issue (My Goodness! I'll explain that to you later), Ronald Bowling.

I forgot what was Ronald's problem. All that I know was that he couldn't urinate properly and he had a tube surgically installed in his body so his kidneys could function and he used a catheter. He had to go to bathroom everyday from time to time. He was a nice kid and he did well in school. Of course, the kids teased him from time to time. In truth, I really didn't bother him. Sometimes, he was annoying but we dealt with him and defended him if any student from other grades that teased him. He just wanted to fit in. Goodness.

Mrs Smith was a tough teacher indeed. Academically, I kept up with her. She was loud and she didn't play either. She would sarcastically put you down on how your performance academically. She already knew about my behavior but she wouldn't hesitate to send me to the "Peace Corner". "He couldn't be still". Sr Saundra was more patient as a principal. She was a "Nun of reasoning". She would talk to you and point out what you did was wrong and strongly believed in the Lord God. However, She and Mrs Smith would come at you when it came to defending Miss Denise Lugo.

Suprisingly, the gang were all growing up. I must say the girls were maturing and they were looking more Woman-like and attractive. Ivy Wright, Sheri Garvin, April Alvarez and Misty. Kelly Giles was still being sassy with her Damn mouth. Us, Boys, it took some time. I, didn't notice that my Body was changing as well, But slowly.

Maurice Thomas tagged along with Vincent and I. I didn't know that he had younger siblings. His younger brother, Willie and his younger sister, Angelice. And He had a hard, stern Father like mine. We called ourselves, "THE THREE MUSKETEERS". Our loyalty was strong indeed. Vincent was more confident and sure of himself. He was Bold and the leader in our clique. But he was sneaky and he was more into sports and chasing the girls. Moreover, He had to prove himself despite being, "short". Maurice was more of a follower of us and looked up to Vincent and I as his "Big Brothers". Now with the Three of us being the best of friends we had to deal with THE FOUR HORSEMEN OF THE APOCALYPSE. Eddie White,

Matt Bradley, Tiecel Mckoy and Kowalski Plummer. They were in the 5th grade and Maurice's younger Brother Willie, tagged along with them. Maurice didn't like those four. I remember he told me that. Every now in then they would crack jokes on us. We defended ourselves in retaliation. I was more laid back and I was happy to have friends though as I was an introvert and Hyper Manic. Honestly, I believed in those two. I strongly believed that I was more loyal out of the three and I was proud to have them as my friends. Derek Sellers already knew Maurice. But "Reese" (as he was called later), and I really had some fun times together.

I was slowly beginning to like the girls more. Anne Carpenter "Woody Wood Pecker" was an adorable antsy little runt she didn't pay attention to me. She did her school work. She was short just as the same height as Misty. She would always tell me, "GET LOST. GET LOST" and walk away or run away in the playground during recess. Little did I know she would get me in some serious trouble later.

Lori Hoskins, I must admit, was more mature out of all the girls that I knew at that school. She recognized my behavior. I guess she was being helpful. I remember that I told her in the 5th Grade that there would be a "New Travis", (quit being silly) and she believed in me. She put confidence in me to the extent that I could sing that lovely song in our spring musical that previous May.

Lori had Auburn hair styled in the early 80's "Facts of Life' and daintly blue eyes. She was just a simple girl aged 11 going on 35. She was more of a woman than the girls and she stood out more in our class. She had more leadership qualities. She didn't have time silliness that's for sure. Hell, she could have been a teacher at St Ann School. But she had a heart. Not one girl has ever made me feel so secure and bringing out the best in me as she did.

As school began as always, I started off good academically then I began slowing down. Progress Reports would be handed out. "Some of y'all better get on the ball" Mrs Smith demanded. She was constantly on me. You see, whenever it came to me, Mrs Smith would immediately get on me. She knew my father would come and get on me. Like the time she took Derek's watch and I took it off from her desk and gave it back to him. "Call His Daddy! Call His Daddy! I'm a get your Daddy on you!" Damn it, then my dad would get on me. Have a conference with Mrs Smith, My Father and I. Daddy would get all hyped up. Going off on me. Eating sweets making him hyper. Anything that happened in class I got blamed for it. As always, I would get in trouble for Stupid Shit.

THE CURSE OF MRS RAFFERTY

Reading Class- We would all be placed in reading groups in class based on our reading level and skills. Houghton Mifflin Company, a reading publishing company that had reading material for children. I was in a group called "Gateways" and I was doing well. BUT unfortunately, there was a mistake. When I was with Mrs Rafferty, "WEAVERS" was a low reading group. Sadly, I failed and she put there that I had to be placed there again. 5th grade class. Just Vincent, Ronald, Jennifer Rathke, Ivy Wright and I had to have class with Mr Toth, (now the 5th grade teacher for reading), that's when we had to deal with THE FOUR HORSEMEN OF THE APOCALYPSE. I was discouraged. Thank you so much, Mrs Rafferty.

Hated being placed in those reading groups. It hurt my self-esteem. Making me feel that I was just useless. That I can't learn and I was so furious. Again, thank you very much Mrs Rafferty.

As for Mrs Smith, we had Math groups. Yes, she would divide the Class based on our skills. I hated those Math groups. And definitely those groups were just senseless. Ridiculous and absurd.

As I said earlier, I was noticing that my Body was changing. I didn't even know about my body odor until Eddie White, Matt Bradley, Tiecel McKoy and Kowalski Plummer with his Bushy Afro. "Musky" they would call me.

"Travis, you need to take a Bath, You smell "Musky" "Stink", said Eddie and putting me down. Matt Bradley would call me "Balooka Head". Tiecel Mckoy and Kowalski would grin and laugh. Even, Mrs Smith would tell the Boys in class that we need to start washing ourselves. She was loud if not anything she would, "I'm a get your Daddy on you!" especially at me. At home, we had two Bathrooms, I did my best washing myself. I used the RIGHT GUARD Deodorant Spray that didn't do any good. One time, Maurice made a little cruel sarcastic remark about me at one time. He had some Balls. Even my cousins on my Father's side made remarks about me being "Stinking". It really made me feel bad. THE FOUR HORSEMEN OF THE APOCALYPSE were the rulers in their class. They crack jokes on you and like I said if those four notice something about you that's not right to them. They would tease you. And they were like that all my last years at that school.

Besides that, I had my Deep Deep Love for music and drawing. It was the mini-series, "Jesus of Nazareth" and as you know the artwork of Richard and Frances Hook. I would draw pictures of Christ through his life, Birth, Crucifixion and subsequent Resurrection. I had my radio in my room. Since, Tonya was attending a new school, Reid Ross Senior High. She was so nervous about some of the girls in our neighborhood. Afraid of getting bullied, But rest assured, They didn't bother her. But Tonya was lucky as a Teenage girl growing up and she had my sister Teasie that would tell her about boys, Sex and menstruation. As for me, Music Appreciation, I liked Prince, The Time and Vanity 6. D-103 FM would play the latest music and I would record my favorite tunes. I loved playing the Drums. Morris Day of the Time was my idol. Wearing those Baggie suits. "WHAT TIME IS IT?" I fell in love with Vanity 6, the late Denise Matthews, the tough talking Brenda Bennett and the innocent Susan Moonsie. I must say this; out of all of Prince's women in his life, Denise Matthews was the most beautiful . Vincent, Maurice and I always talked about them. Prince exploded in the 80's, Michael Jackson and Madonna established a strong pop culture impact on the youth in the little town of Fayetteville, NC. Everybody wanted to wear some Baggies or a Baggie suit. Craig Douglas and I went to a Clothing store downtown and they had all the Baggie Suit and Stacy Adams shoes. All colors you name it. Craig dressed his best at Reid Ross because he graduated in '83. Well, I had only one pair of

Baggies, they were gray but I wanted more. I had penny loafers and black dress shoes. My Father told my that Grandfather "PK" was a well dressed man and he wore a Stetson Hat and Stacy Adams.

Getting back to school, Mrs Smith would not play when it comes to grades. When it's time for report cards, I would get so nervous to show them to my Dad. I had a reputation for "lying". I would lie over anything. But my Family wouldn't have none of it. So one time during our second nine weeks, I was given my report card. It wasn't that good at all. So what I did was make "B's for the "F's. Little did I know I would always get caught. Mrs Smith knew I did that. Thinking that she accomplished anything but she didn't. End of Story.

"Call his Daddy!" "I'm a get your Daddy on you". "Where your Daddy at?" That what all she would say.

Our Den Mother was Danielle Ely's Mother. Mrs Ely was such a Joy. She made me feel so jubilant. I was so fond of her. She very Kind and she always get on me. She disciplined me but she went along with the flow with me. A very nice woman. I adored her very much.

But back at home, My Family was in a crisis. My mother was having serious mental struggles. Tonya sensed that. Mom would just go off and yelling. Teasie came home from Florida to see our mother in sorrow. My parents got into serious arguments about some issues in our Family that I can't share with you. My Father's mother "Grandmother Meta" had died early March 1983. The funeral was held at the Shiloh Church of Christ in Eastover. All my cousins sat to the left side of the church. A few of them cried. A very, very sad funeral. Indeed. My father's Siblings grieved deeply. Especially my Father, He took it really hard. It was the first time, I ever had seen my father cry. So sad and broken.

But our troubles as a Family weren't over. My Grandmother "Daisy" came by the house to see her daughter. My mother was so worn out. I just thought that she was just tired. She was in the living room. I slowly approached to her, "Ma are you alright?" She had her Head down and she looked up at me and answered softly, "I'm tired, Travis."

This was my mother's first mental breakdown. She got the treatment and was diagnosed Bipolar Manic Depressive. The doctor that treated her was Dr Gomez. My mother never returned to work for awhile. Both of my parents Families knew about the crisis we were in and they didn't interfere. Eventually, we pulled through.

Spring -1983. School was the same old thing. That March there was bad wintry weather and It snowed really bad. We were out of school for several days. Spring came slowly and it blossomed.

THE OUTSIDERS. A novel written by S.E. Hinton. The story focuses on gangs in her native Oklahoma. It was a Major motion Picture Directed by Francis Ford Coppola. He directed, THE GODFATHER and APOCALYPSE NOW. It starred teen Heart throbs Matt Dillion, C. Thomas Howell, Ralph Macchio, Rob Lowe, Tom Cruise, Emilio Estevez and Patrick Swayze. Most of the girls in my Class were Crazy and in Love with all of them. So did, Tonya. I went to the movies with my sister's husband. Teasie got married last year 1982. John Tucker came along with me to go see it. It was shown at the Cross Creek Cinema. In class we read a small play adapted from the book. A very good Film. You can have sympathy for the Greasers, poor kids as some of the members get in trouble. The Soc's were the arrogant "preppy gang" that looked down on them. The music composed by Carmine Coppola is so inspiring. "Stay Gold" so beautifully sung by the great Stevie Wonder. I fell in love with that song.

Since, we were near the end of the School, I went to the Bazzar, all by myself. It was held on the last Saturday of April of all things. I do remember Maurice playing a trick on me by sending me to jail for a few minutes. It was part of games that you play. And I was suprised to see Vincent being there. Somehow, to be honest, I was very Hyper Manic, but not too "Wild", I would say. Eventually, I joined my fellow "MUSKETEERS". It was a great day. But this one Festival was different. I wasn't there all that day but it was crowded.

I got home that day. Tonya was boiling some Hot Dogs and frying French Fries. Tonya told me to look after the food while it was cooking. Tonya and I were listening to our record player. We had a collection of albums. Prince, The Time, Vanity 6, The DeBarge and Michael Jackson's THRILLER. Dad was taking a Bath. So, the last time I was checking on the food in the kitchen. I went back to Tonya's room. We were listening to the DEBARGE tune, "Stop Don't Tease Me". Until, All of a sudden there was darkness like a dark cloud was coming in Tonya's room. "It looks like it's going to rain", I said. To this day, If I didn't go to that kitchen when I saw Fire and black smoke in the Kitchen. I panicked. The flames blazing on the cabinets and on the over. I yelled, "Tonya, the kitchen's on fire!!" Tonya got up and our Dog Pooh-Bear was barking wildly and excited as Tonya tried to put out the flames. I ran out of the house yelling, "Fire!'. And we called Dad, who was still taking a Bath. He quickly got out of the tub. Put on his towel wrapped around his waist to put out the fire frantically. Our neighbor across the street James came and tried to help us out. "You're Alright, Mr. Hodges". He put out the fire. I was already outside in our Back Yard. Tonya ran too. The fire didn't damage that much to our Kitchen. Just the oven and our two conjoined cabinets. Smoke was everywhere. Tonya and I were in our Backyard looking worried and concerned. Dad eventually came out of the house. He just went off. "This don't make no Damn sense." Highly Upset at us. So, Dad and Tonya returned to the kitchen to clean what the fire had damaged to our kitchen. Dad was arguing and Tonya was quiet as she helped him cleaning what was left. Me? I was still outside in our Backyard. Yet, there was one person I was so worried about: my Mother.

Mom came home from Shopping at Cross Creek Mall as she parked the Gray Regal into our patio. I was nervous as hell when she walked into the house. Much to my suprise....She was calm. Dad and Tonya explained to my mother was happened. I returned to the house. I thought for sure that I was in for it. But my parents knew that it was Tonya's fault who caused that fire. She wasn't watching the food as she was cooking. Few Days later, our Kitchen was repaired. Brand new. Just one time, Mom brought it up and argued with me about it. I kept my mouth shut. I {SIGHED] and went to my room. End of Story.

At school, Field Day came as usual. Spring was very beautiful in May. Our class participated, But the thing was we had to have a team name for ourselves. Mrs Smith asked us what should call ourselves. I suggested, "The 6th grade 76'ers" Vincent agreed. He said, "I like that." My classmates couldn't come to an accordance. So, Matt Vaughan suggested, "The Smurfs". All the Class liked that. I sure as Hell didn't. It pissed me off. We made a poster sign using our crayons and markers. Well, as the event began, we were teased and laughed by the other classes outside. Especially, THE FOUR HORSEMEN OF THE APOCALYPSE, shit they'll laugh at any damn thing.

We didn't have to wear our customary uniforms. We wore regular clothes. The girls were wearing t-shirts and shorts with their developing bodies. Vincent was excited as hell. His hormones were already kicking. The girls were growing up and looking attractive. Lori Hoskins, Kelly Giles, April Alvarez, Danielle Ely, Ivy Wright, Sheri Garvin with her dark brunette hair waved back 80's style looking like being in a punk band. I really saw the change in her. She was being rebellious.

Sex Education was taught in class during this time. But we already knew about it. Mrs Smith knew as silly as I was in class she couldn't deal with me at times she sent me to Sr Saundra's office about my behavior. My father didn't really talk to me about sex and girls. He mentioned it with our work book. Unfortunately, He never told about relationships between men and women. Marriage and Divorce. He just didn't give me the real talk about Sex and Women. He knew that I was growing up but, honestly, I think he didn't have the time to tutor me about the pros and cons of life.

Now, as the Field Day was taking place. I wanted us to cheer and have fun. Mrs Smith wasn't having it. She sent me to wall outside while the kids were having fun. Here I go again.

The last day of school was approaching, I was really worried. I gave my all in my school work. My performance was much better than 5th grade, I could tell you that. So, A Kick Ball Game was planned with us (the Smurfs) against the 5th grade (THE FOUR HORSEMEN OF THE APOCALYPSE) were ready to play us.

Last Day of School was a cloudy chilly day but the blue sky appeared later that day. We were given our report cards. I passed to the 7th grade and yes I was happy! It was like a long exhale. My classmates talking and saying farewells. I thought I was going to California to visit my sister Teasie who was still in the Navy. There was talk about spending the summer of '83 in California. It never happened.

THE SUPER BOWL. So, the game was taking place. I must say it was very serious game. Vincent and I, were devoted to that game because we knew how good, (THE FOUR HORSEMEN OF THE APOCALYPSE) were. Oh, they were ready to play kickball against us. Tensions were already growing between them and Vincent, Maurice and I the whole year. They were picking on us. Fights were about happen. The playground was all ours. To make a very long historic game short. It was like the Super Bowl, Believe me. It was no joke. April Alvarez was ready to play too. As a tough girl as she was, She played right along with us. Mike Ortiz performed very well. He was good. Matt Bradley was an outstanding kicker on the opposing team. He played Soccer. Whenever it was his turn, Vincent, Maurice and I had to spread out. Matt could kick that Ball straight out to busy traffic street to the cemetery on Grove Street. Eddie, Kowalski and Tiecel played well. Ivy Wright, Angela Butler and Danielle Ely were more the cheerleaders for us. We got teased being called, "The Smurfs" but we were Bad. "Some Smurfs we are!" yelled Danielle being cheerfully. Luckily, The 5th grade won the game. Barely. We were crushed. But I was upset with Maurice. We argued a little bit because I didn't think he was giving his best in the field. Vincent Robinson and I had experience dealing with, (THE FOUR HORSEMEN OF THE APOCALYPSE), We played against them since 3rd grade along with Sean Lane. He was gone but we could've won. I was upset. We all returned to class. Willie Thomas (Maurice's younger Brother), came by our class and wished us a good game we all played. So, I went to the 5th grade class and did the same. Kowalski Plummer yelled, "GOOD GAME TRAV!" and I shooked his hand and few kids in the class. And I didn't want to be a sore loser. I looked at that game to summarize it up. The winners were the losers and the losers were the winners. The game was tensed, hard but enjoyable. Well, it was the last Day of School. Finally, I can enjoy a Full summer.

Summer of '83 was lots of fun. Dad took Tonya and I to the movies and we saw the conclusion of George Lucas' sci-fi epic Trilogy, STAR WARS EPISODE VI : RETURN OF THE JEDI. Everybody was wondering about the shocking revelation to the defeated Luke Skywalker from the Evil Darth Vader at the end of their Lightsaber duel. Also that summer, We saw SUPERMAN III. It was okay. Superman exposed to the Kryptonite that turns him to a "GASP!" A Bad Guy. OH NO! The villain was Brainiac and comedian Richard Pryor starred in this one. After his burning accident, I was glad he pulled through. Clark Kent reuniting with Lana Lang at his High school Reunion at Smallville, Kansas. But Christopher Reeve was comical as the "Evil Superman". But he saves the day by battling within himself. The Evil Superman and The Good Superman "You always wanted fly to Kent. Now's your Chance!." Good always prevail and Superman saves the Day with a little help from Pryor. I listened more of Prince and the Time. Tonya and I would watch Music Videos on NBC, "Friday Night Videos". Mom would take Tonya and I to the Tyler's News and Camera Shop every Sunday to buy the latest in Magazines and paperback novels of all kinds. RIGHT ON!, BLACK BEAT and Tonya would buy her magazine, SEVENTEEN. Getting latest scoop about Prince and Tonya was in love with the Family Singing group, DEBARGE. James DeBarge was her favorite when they were popular in the music scene. Her "Crush" on James. She would buy two copies of Right On! I forgot that issue with all of them on the cover. Mom loved getting her 'SOUTHERN LIVING' magazine. That was her favorite. Michael Jackson's "THRILLER" Album was still killing and climbing on Billboard Charts. THE BOTTOM was always THE BOTTOM. I was listening to on my Walk Man cassette player and reading my magazines about Prince but I never heard anything about the Time. I was so excited to learn that Prince is planning a

MOVIE. But Where's The TIME? Later that year, I would get the biggest shock of my life.

Late, August-1983. 7th grade. So, Let's get the shit started, Miss Lugo was my teacher. We had few new students. Christopher Franklin, Morgan Hardwick (Okay Girls, Start Screaming!), Loretta Dempsey, Jenny Chriss and Kim Micheaux (wild and disrespectful). Misty Balsamo, Mike Ortiz and Sheri Garvin attended Pine Forrest Junior High. Kelly Giles, Genevieve Beateau and Lori Hoskins never returned. I was expecting Lori to return but she didn't. She left.... Vincent Robinson left to attend Lewis Chapel Middle School. Well, since Vincent left, THE THREE MUSKETEEERS remained an outfit. It also drew Maurice Thomas and I closer as friends. Still, we called each other on the phone from time to time and touching base. We would go to the Skating Rink at EUTAW VILLAGE. Constantly, Maurice and I had to deal with "THE FOUR HORSEMEN OF THE APOCALYPSE".

Ronald Bowling was becoming a nuisance to the class this time. Miss Lugo always defended him and if you say anything about him you'll be in trouble. He got me in trouble and I didn't know what it was about. Ronald was annoying and I had to apologize to him. But I was so incensed to tell you the truth I wanted to Grab Him!! GRRR!! Miss Lugo sensed that I was growing up and of course, my hormones was really kicking. We were all growing up. Boys and Girls growing up. My Hyper Manic demeanor was highly kicking because my Crush on Miss Lugo was still on point but towards the end of the year I was getting into real serious trouble. Mrs Smith and Sr Saundra, was always present to defend and protect her when it came to me. Also, it was the new discipline action being taken place.

The CONDUCT REFERRAL. A document that informs the student and their parents about the acts committed in class that is brought attention to by the Teacher. You're given a total of Five and you will be expelled indefinitely.

The First – is given to the student by the Teacher just to remind and informs the student about his/her actions committed in class.

The Second – is given to the student and parents By the Teacher to inform you're being warned and it is discussed with them.

The Third – You will be having a conference with the Teacher and Principal with the student and their parents.

The Fourth – There will be a conference with the Teacher, the student, the Parents, the Principal and the Pastor. The Final Warning. (You're in Hot Water).

The Fifth and Final Referral- Expulsion from the School will take place. (Hell, I received all of them). The Uncontrollable Child.

My crush with Ms Lugo was making Headlines everywhere in school. But it was getting out of control. I would do the, "Mr. Gomez Addams love For Morticia" kissing on Miss Lugo. "Mushy Mushy" that I would say. And I would do a little dancing thing. The class would laugh. It made me happy But I did that before in the fourth Grade. Until the End, Miss Lugo was getting frustrating, annoyed and not tolerating it all. I strongly believed she wanted me out as well.

By the time as school began we were in those Damn reading groups. I was placed in "BANNERS", after I finished "WEAVERS". Mrs Smith was teaching the reading classes so I had to go the 8th grade classroom and for the Damn Math Class. Now, get this, Mrs Smith had me separated from class. Moved my desk to her desk so she can keep her eye on me. But, "THE FOUR HORSEMEN OF THE APOCALYPSE" was there. Yes, I was clowning around. Mrs Smith would not only get on me but a few others in class. Don't forget she was sarcastic as well to the class. I think that this was around the time, Mrs Smith and Miss Lugo became a clique. When it came to me, they got each others back. We had a new student, Morgan Hardwick (Girls Scream!), A lean, blonde haired, handsome kid, which blew some of the girls minds. Just about all the girls had, "Big Time Crushes" on him. He was quiet as first but when it came to us he fit in with us. "A smart Alec", he wasn't afraid of, "THE FOUR HORSEMEN OF THE APOCALYPSE". Various times, He stood up to them. Morgan and I got along pretty well. In some ways, he was a mature kid out of the Boys is concerned. It didn't take long for him to notice me and my manic antics. He lived with his grandparents, who were so friendly and lovable. I enjoyed them, dearly.

Miss Lugo had a little party for us. We brought our tapes and records. I brought my album, "1999" by Prince, a masterpiece. We had fun But when started the party, Sr Mary Phyllis had this talk with me because she taught music as well and she was talking to me that I was being watched and they felt I didn't deserve to be on the Basketball Team. I didn't care. I returned to class. Since it was alike a 'Talent Show'. Forrest was the DJ and played the records on our little record player. I wanted perform "Little Red Corvette". I lip synch. I didn't sing it while the music was playing. Miss Lugo was really looking foward to me performing it. I didn't sing the whole song. The Music Video, I tried to imagine myself being Prince. April and Danielle were screaming. Rooting for me. I tried to dance and I clumsily tried to do a split and I hurt myself. Miss Lugo was terrified and looked in shocked. I was laughed at. I felt I let the class down.

BASKETBALL TEAM

I wanted to be in the basketball team and I tried out and made it. Well, this is where things in my life was like a Damn rollercoaster, Believe me and It all focused on me.

November-1983, Miss Jacobs, the 6th grade teacher. A Whale who's been mad at the world because of it. She taught Science and Art. Mr Toth was still the 5th grade teacher. He was the coach last year. Practise started in November. Yes, I was overly excited or manically excited. BUT!!! Your Grades has to be good and you have to keep them up. I forgot the name of the two coaches that helped us but it doesn't matter anyway. I tried my best. Maurice was furious that he didn't make it on the team.

To top it off. As a field trip we went to Raleigh to the NC Museum of Art. Before that, since I received a Progress report on my grade on Science and I made a 73=D. Well, I didn't want my father to know so what I did? I forged my father's signature on the report. So, on that Sunday, Miss Jacobs called my home and told my dad about it. He approached me and I thought I was going to get it. I went to my room. This was the First Conduct Referral. Matt Vaughan was suspended from School by Miss Lugo, I didn't know why. He was constantly getting in trouble with her. Giving him shit. So, after, the trip when we returned to class. Before school was over that day, Miss Jacobs gave me the letter which was the Conduct Referral. I had a feeling what it was. When I came home and gave it to my Dad. He was furious and I asked him what it was about though I knew what is was. "It's about what you did. Forging my name!!" my Dad said furiously. It got worse. The next day after school, Sr Saundra approached to me and gave me another letter stating that I was on probation and I was longer on the Basketball team. She took me off of the team. And gave another letter explaining what I done. The teachers gave their honest opinions on me. But, it was Sr Mary Phyllis , the only one supportive of me about this Christmas play that I was so interested and excited to partake. So, I came home feeling miserable and caught hell by my parents. Dad lectured me that night enough of that story.

THE GREAT LATE POTENTATE, A Children's Christmas Musical. Written by Karen Dean and Produced by Greg Nelson. The hero Jasper, A jolly, arrogant and kind Moorish king with full aristocracy, who "journeyed cross the desert sands, through raging storms and robber bands" who followed the Three Magi after the Star of Bethlehem disappeared. And when he arrived there in Bethlehem, he encounters some Children Shepherds who tells him about the infant Christ they saw and how it was so wonderful that baby's mother Mary let them look at him and touched him. But as for poor Jasper, He was "Late"and he had a "Gift" for the Christ Child. It was broken and "I can't give a Broken gift to a King". But the Children explained to him it doesn't matter because, "With Jesus, it's never too late". He was THE GIFT. So, with despair and sadness, the children insists that if he wanted to see the Christ Child, "Follow Him". At the end, He leaves Bethlehem and gives his farewell to the Children as he seeks out the infant Christ.

Auditions were being held at the Social Hall My class encouraged me to do it. The kids knew that role was meant for me. Like I said, my classmates knew my behavior. So as the auditions were done. Sr Mary Phyllis announced the cast members and I was the leading cast member. I was excited and somewhat suprised. Everyone rooted for me. Nothing could stop me because I wanted to do the Best as JASPER!

The play was directed Mrs Wallace and Mrs Eanes. Very kind and thoughtful women. Mrs Wallace had a daughter named Janice who was casted in the play. The cast included Lia Shorter, Matt Vaughn, Ronald Bowling, Kim Michaeux, Janice Wallace, Amy Goodwin and a few others.

I was afraid and nervous because I didn't know the lyrics to all of the songs. I was thinking about since I was cut from the Basketball team, I feel that I had to prove myself to everybody there. I kept up with my work during the rehearsals. Mrs Smith kept reminding me. I wanted to do the best that I could. During that time I spoked with Sr Saundra, the "Nun of reasoning" at the Social Hall and she explained on what she had to do. I was feeling resentful still. But, she called me, "The Great Late Travis McLaurin". During my, "THE GREAT LATE POTENTATE" days I was given a button pin. The den mothers was made a costume for me and cast members. It was a Black Russian Hat like crown, a Purple robe and I chose my blue sweat pants. Wearing white socks with a sandals. I looked like a real clown.

The musical was performed on the cold evening of December 1983. We did two performances. One for the students and the final performance was that night. I was highly "Manic". We gave our all and we did the Best. However, I was the Star of the Show, I was given a standing ovation. I wanted everyone to be proud of me.

As, I look back on this momentous occasion, I was making a prophecy. That Night, there were few people who saw me who I was revealing myself. As far as my classmates, they probably knew that I had something to give. I was on top of the World. A child of thirteen, I felt I was rising and that God Almghty was Blessing me as if Jasper Struggled trying to find the infant Christ who had just been born. He wasn't there and he was still searching for the star. As he proclaimed himself, " I AM THE GREAT" and the Children point out at him, "LATE!!!" and he responds proudly, "POTENTATE!!"

Christmas Holidays was usual. On the Sunny Bitter Cold Sunday. My parents quickly prepared a fire in our little Fireplace in the den. Tonya and I got more clothes than toys. I got a little guitar but I wanted a set of Drums. No STAR WARS. Those toys were Expensive back then. Christmas was usual in the McLaurin household. But there one thing that we got something we never thought we would get. CABLE TV. Our television screen was looking very clear as ever. All of the kids in Class had HBO way before me.

Returning to school. New Year. 1984. Feeling Confident as ever, "THE GREAT LATE POTENTATE", I was slowly experiencing "Mood Swings". I do remember Morgan Hardwick saying, "Travis is in his MOODS." I was still struggling with my Behavior and there was no suprise for Ms Lugo, she was getting engaged. It didn't really bother me at all, honestly. I was constantly acting a clown like "MR T!" Yes, I did. I could do a good impression of him. He was a clown, to me. As I explaining about my symptoms of my behavior, Mrs Smith and Ms Lugo was getting highly upset. I was still doing the "MUSHY MUSHY" on Ms Lugo. You could tell that my crush was landing me in trouble. One afternoon, afterschool, Maurice Thomas was talking to me by those steel monkey Bars at the playground and warning me. "You keep on messing with her. You're going to be getting those Conduct Referrals." He cautioned me but I didn't listened. By this time, The Conduct referral was up for grabs. Real stupid shit. I don't think I was a "BULLY". I wasn't a bully. A Bully is a person that is habitually cruel to smaller people. Pick Fights. Yes, I did tease and I will admit to that but there were those who was "Wild" as I. I wasn't perfect at all. But I was quickly getting into more trouble as a result of my behavior. The Conduct Referrals were coming. The second was over that little fuck Ronald. Ms Burke, our physical education teacher, was thinking that I was teasing him but I wasn't. I never cared too much for her. She always tried to make me feel worthless.She was always against me. The third one was quick and fast really stupid as hell. I kicked Ann Carpenter in the hallway as the Whale Ms Jacobs accused me of. Yes, I wanted to but I didn't hurt her at all. My leg didn't even hit Her!! Anne Carpenter could have stood up for me. The Fourth one resulted in my Hatred for Ms Lugo. I strongly Believed, it was a set up. Angela Butler and Danielle Ely stabbed me in my back. Very Very Stupid. I was talking with them in Social Studies Class to them about the movie, "ANNIE" that was recently shown on HBO. I was only just joking with them. After Social Studies in Sr Mary Phyllis' Class, when we returned to class as Ronald was consulted for name calling me and a few others. Before Lunch, I'll never forget that day, Angela and Danielle went straight to Miss Lugo with their arms folded and said something like, "He did it."And Ms Lugo nodded her head. And the Fourth Conduct Referral was done by none other than Miss Denise Lugo. I was in the principal's office. Sr Saundra talked to me. Stressing that you've been warned about your conduct in class. I was getting nervous or I guess you would say paranoid. Now, Ms Lugo had the advantage that she didn't know that this was my fourth conduct Referral. She had Mrs Smith and Sr Saundra were on alert to protect Ms Lugo from any student in her class. When she gave me that letter and Maurice saw it and he looked at me with a sly smile as if to say, "I told you."

It was getting tensed in class that time. The Boys and Girls were at it with each other. All the boys were getting in trouble. It was a like a volcano about to erupt. So, Maurice and Forrest started this, "Womens Haters Club". I was for it. We had one meeting during recess talking about Ms Lugo. It was just only for the Boys in the Seventh Grade. And, I was dealing and I was about to get in a Fight with, "THE FOUR HORSEMEN OF THE APOCALYPSE". Calling me, "MUSKY, Trav, YOU SMELL MUSKY!". Miss Lugo pulled me to the side at class telling me that I have a body odor and Sr Mary Phyllis did the same. I was getting self conscious of myself.

My discordance with Ms Lugo was rising. Not only I was having trouble with her. Derek Sellers, Matt Vaughn And Morgan Hardwick was having their time with her. I was trying to keep myself out of Trouble. At one time, I thought I wanted to be "Saved" and calming myself down. Being a Born-Again Christian that didn't work at all. I was getting nowhere with that. It suprised my Class Because they knew my behavior. I felt like a DAMN FOOL, walking with my orange Bible. You have to be really dedicated to be a born-again. Then all of a sudden, The Class was against me. Maurice and I were having some altercations. Partly, it had to do with that warning. And he was calling me, "MUSKY and FLABBY". We got into it. So, I challenged Maurice to a Fight in the Boys Room.

After, Social Studies Class, Forrest Alvarez, Chris Franklin, Matt Vaughan and I think Morgan wasn't there to witness it. We went in the Boys Room. I remember Forrest was like the referee Official.

And he hid under the sink. So, Maurice and I stared at each other. We exchanged a few words. I remember saying to him, "What did you Say?" and Maurice was at the corner. Then, the fight was on. It lasted not a minute. I was just throwing punches and Maurice was trying hold and grab my arms. Strangling me. Trying to block my intended blows. I do remember I hit him hard on his head and he just only got just a small punch on my chin and that was it. The Boys broke up the Fight. I quickly walk out of the restroom and I was Full of rage. And I came back in, We almost got into it again. Maurice wasn't afraid as they pulling him back. And we went back to Class.

Word spreaded quick in Class, Travis and Maurice were fighting. Chris Franklin, our last new student in class talked it about during Lunch. He was hyped up telling Kim Micheaux about it. He was saying that I was Falling down and Maurice Won. They both laughed. A rematch was set after Lunch at recess.

The came recess. The fight was supposed to be held behind the Social Hall. All the girls, April, Danielle, Angela, Ivy and that ridiculous silly Kim Micheaux ran to see what was about to happen. Everybody in our class circled around us and was ready to see the rematch. I was getting a little nervous because I got Four Conduct referrals. I was ready and Maurice had no fear. He was ready too. Now, being a soft person, I knew that I was going to get Expelled this time for real. We looked at each other. We were ready to go at it again. I mentioned Vincent to him and said, "You know Vincent wouldn't want this." Then, I extended my hand to say peace. Maurice looked at me the same way. He didn't say and I think he was thinking the same thing too. It never happened. We both shook hands. Everybody was disappointed but saying, "AWWWW, They made up". I was feeling embarrassed. I was angry still. However, if we were at anyplace besides the school campus it would have been on. Believe me. Recess was over. The Kids talked about Travis and Maurice didn't fight and made up. Alex Ewing, who was sitting next to me and she said, "I heard you and Maurice made up". I didn't say anything. I was quiet that whole day.

Srping – 1984. We already yearning for the School Year to end.

We were some Damn "Clowns". The Girls were looking attractive. I caught my eye on April Alvarez. Dressing "Preppy" like all the girls when we didn't have to wear our uniforms. But it was Lori Hoskins that I still thought about. I really missed her. HBO was the Big thing. Having cable TV. We were all talking about the Videos and music and Ms Lugo still let us play our records. She was a big Music Lover. And She loved the DeBarge hit song, "Time will Reveal" and "Queen of My heart" with Kim Micheaux. If you're a Girl name your Favorite DeBarge member: Randy, Mark, Eldra and James. This Time I sung the sung before class. "THE GREAT LATE POTENTATE" was Back! School was about to end that day. The Girls were having their crushes on Morgan Hardwick but out of the Girls He really liked was Danielle Ely. I remember He talked about to me about her alot. I was teased by him and Ivy Wright, "Travis, You're Wild!".

Bazzar- May 1984. It was a Beautiful Saturday. The Food. Arts and Craft. Mrs Wallace was there. I must say she was one of the most kind ladies that I ever come across Along with Mrs Ely and Mrs Senninger, the mother of my classmate, John Senninger. She and Lots of the Kids wanted me to perform a few songs from, "THE GREAT LATE POTENTATE. I did. Ms Burke, the PE teacher was hosting a game and she had a microphone and she announced, 'Travis is going to sing a song". The music teacher who played the piano on our musical, I forgot her name. UGHH!! I sung, "THE GIFT" I was given the microphone. It was a very crowded. I was nervous because I was afraid of not remembering the lyrics But I sung the song and it came naturally. A Big Applause. Lots of people were there at this one. In the Social Hall, there lots of games. "THE FOUR HORSEMEN OF THE APOCALYPSE" were present, of course. It was a good day. This one out of all the Bazzars that I went was probably the best. I enjoyed it. I was more appreciated than ever.

Morgan Hardwick and Ivy Wright were more leaders in our class especially when we passed to the Eighth Grade. They talked the talk and walked the walk. I, being manic as hell, I just wanted to be friends with everyone. The Last Day of School, June 1984. There was a Pizza Party the day before. We had a Singing contest Ronald Bowling and I. We had to be sentimental and sympathetic to him because we did protect him. He sung Michael Jackson's "BEAT IT". And I must say he was really into it. We rooted for him. I tried to sing, Lionel Ritchie's "Hello". And "Baby stay with me tonight" by Jeffrey Osbourne. I let him have it but he did sound very good. Basically, it was in some ways a farewell. Because, Danielle Ely was leaving. Just about all the kids in our Class were leaving. Military Kids. Morgan, I must say was crazy about Danielle. He didn't want her to leave. I have to say this Day, in my opinion. If there were only Kids in my class that I see being a married couple and having Children. Michael Ortiz and Kelly Giles. Morgan Hardwick and Danielle Ely. Enough Said.

That day was emotional for us. We took photos. Ms Lugo had her camera and she took of all of us. We played music. The kids socialized and we just had fun. There was something Miss Lugo had made a comment to me. Mind you, it was not offensive but I'll never forget. She said, "I'll never stop liking you, Travis". The whole class gave expressions, "WHOOOOOO!" and I wasn't really all that concerned but I never understood it. I didn't care. Ms Lugo had high expectations for me. We were given our report cards and we all passed as I mentioned earlier. I was kind of hurt especially Danielle Ely was leaving for California and Anne Carpenter, said that she was moving to Colorado. We said our farewells and Angela Butler was crying. All of the kids were leaving but my resentment towards Ms Lugo has already been slowly and It was going to be WAR. This was just the beginning of my Struggle and ordeal. It was my interim that I would be terribly and cruelly persecuted. It was the beginning of the Stigma of my having a disease in my Brain that affected my behavior. As I preached it that night in December 1983 at our Christmas Musical, "I've journeyed cross the deserts sands. Through Raging storms and Robber bands. I sought this place long after, the star had disappeared."

That summer of 1984, I became an uncle. My nephew, Dante' was born three months earlier in March. Tonya and I were so excited. Partly, that the new film Prince starred called, "PURPLE RAIN".

I had my deep love of Art, music and wanting to play the drums. I would listen to beat to the Music I listened to all kinds of music. Seriously, I inherited that from my Father. He has a love of Classical Music, Folk, and of course Soul music. He had a Broad mind because his siblings were tolerate of him watching, TCHIAKOVSY'S "THE NUTCRAKER" on Television back in Christmas 1987 at our house. That Summer, alot was going on in "THE BOTTOM". Tonya just turned seventeen and I turned fourteen.

PURPLE RAIN was the movie that premiered in July 1984 directed by Albert Magnoli. The TIME was back despite Morris Day's friction and Drama with Prince and the Revolution. MTV threw a party for the film at Mann's Chinese Theater in Hollywood. Vanity 6 was renamed and Apollonia 6, There was interviews. I wished that I was there. Patricia "Apollonia" Kotero was so beautiful along with Brenda and Susan. Morris Day was cool wearing his White Baggy suit as ever but the thing was; WE NEVER HEARD PRINCE TALK! I already had a clue how his voice was sounded like and listening to his Albums. When there were clips of the Film of him talking to Apollonia "to pass the waters of Lake Minnetonka". And Tonya had a FIT!! "That's how he talk??!!." Apollonia strips her Black leather outfit down to her panties. And she innocently jumps into the lake and "The Kid" tells her, "That's not Lake Minnetonka". End of story. He just wanted to see her naked and how far he could test her. The Album was the most played Album on the Radio. Everywhere. We followed that phenomena Up and Down. And we received Better Cable. A Box and a Remote Control!! There were all the channels we had, USA Network, ESPN, CNN and SHOWTIME. We saw PURPLE RAIN with John and Teasie. A Great Cinematic experience But I wanted to go see, INDIANA JONES AND THE TEMPLE OF DOOM but there were reviews was mixed. Saying it was bloody and gory. It was one of the first films to almost receive a PG-13 rating.

We bought the Albums and 12-inch Singles at Paradise Records and Cassette Tapes on McPherson Church Road. We had to sneak our records to the other side of the house to Tonya's room Because

Dad will have a Fit when it comes to purchasing Magazines and Records. We always had to do that for awhile. Dad didn't even liked it when we watched MTV 24/7 (Chuckle). MTV (Music Television) was for the generation of Teens and Young Adults who loved to see their favorite artists videos and music specials. Over the years, especially in the 80's decade, MTV was a popular scene that defined a popular culture All over the countries all over the world in music and entertainment.

1984 was arguably the Year for Prince, I must say. Everything from being on MTV News to premiere Videos, despite the competing record sales of Michael Jackson's THRILLER and Madonna's LIKE A VIRGIN. Then, there was a "New" Appreciation for Classical composer, Mozart. 'AMADEUS', a fictional-biography film directed by Milo Forman focusing on the genius of the late Austrian maestro seen through the eyes of a jealous rival Antonio Saleri. My Dad was so excited, at first I thought he wanted to go see it.

I delved myself more in Music, Arts and Films than ever before. I had a little Walkman-Cassette Tape player. And I had a collection of Tapes from Prince and the TIME. Tonya and I had quite a Collection of Albums. And we were going to continue to collect them from now on. No matter what. I wish that I had a set of drums like Bobby Z, the drummer in Prince's Band the Revolution. I would get two wooden sticks and just beat away on our green Plastic Trash Can and Sing to myself to songs from Prince and the TIME. "777-9311" was the song I was so obsessed with. I would listen to that "BEAT" up and down. I know that "Beat" to this Day and I would analyze it to you-The Right way. I was an annoyance to my Daddy and at School. Using my pencils and just drum away. I always made "beats" from my head. Mrs Smith, once said to me in class, "I wish I get you a drum set and play them outside". My Father would say, "Stop that Beatin, Boy!" Because we had to be quiet in our den as Dad was sleeping during the Day and he would go to work the Night Shift.

My parents had some quirky Hours when they were working at Kelly Springfield (now, GoodYear). I knew that my mother would mostly work 2nd Shift for a Long time when I started attending St

Ann's. Sometimes, I wouldn't see her until the weekends. Dad had to work Morning Shift or Night shift which I hated. From the time I was in the 3rd Grade to I left St Ann's, he was on those quirky Shifts. He would be in his moods. He would get up from Bed and walked to the Bathroom. He had an Evil look on his Face. I know there plenty of times Dad didn't get any sleep at all. He had his ways and Maurice's Father, knew my Father's ways. Enough Said.

Also, at the End of Summer - My Dad's youngest Sister, Bronnie Williams would always throw Family Cookouts at her house in Eastover. We were always invited to come, of course. I would meet my cousins. But the Food was Galore. Fried Fish, Hamburgers, Hot Dogs, Cole slaw, Fried Chicken. There was a pool that my Uncle David purchased and it was fun. I wanted to swim but I was afraid to. My Cousins, Preston, Todd and Marc, Bronnie's daughters, Natasha, Tameka and their little brother "PV" enjoyed swimming in the pool. What made this one very special was that my Mother came with us. Feeling better with good Spirits, she was treated with kindness and love by everyone, including my Father's sisters Christine, Lois and His Brother, Dan Wesley. And my sister, Teasie's firstborn son, my nephew, Dante'.

My last school year at St Ann School. August 1984. Orientation Day. Over those summer months, My resentment towards Ms Lugo was set in motion. I didn't want to see her or talk to her for that matter. This year, she was teaching the 5th grade. Because of those Conduct referrals I was given I felt it was unfair. Especially that Fourth one. So, the last Friday of that Eighth Month. It was fairly hot that day. I walked and entered the school and I was greeted with respect by Lorena Shepard's youngest Brother Andy, "Hi Travis." As he greeted and walked past me in the hall. I was so suprised. As I walked down the hall. Maurice was there and a few others in my class were there. Ms Lugo was talking to some parents in her new designed classroom. And she was wearing a DRESS. A Purple Dress!! A complete Surprise! Ms Lugo hated Dresses but I think that She going through a "New Look" about herself. She caught sight of me. I tried to avoid her as much as I could. As, I was walking into the 7th grade class She caught sight of me, I had my head slightly down and she saw me. Miss Lugo, was happy that day and I think she expected me to go to her class and talk to her. But I didn't want to. She was sensing the growing tensions between the both of us.

School began at my last year. It was just a regular day. I was really irritable. Partly, Because We had a joint Class with the 7th Grade, in one room. With "THE FOUR HORSEMEN OF THE APOCALYPSE". And Eddie White always had a way with the girls. They were in Charge of their crew. Mrs Smith was our teacher. Both classes were small. Sr Mary Phyllis, Mr Toth and Miss Jacobs left. My Class was just only nine of us. Angela Butler, Chris Franklin, Morgan Hardwick, David Lee, Derek Sellers, Lorena Shepard, Maurice Thomas, Ivy Wright and I. Yes, Mrs Smith had me sit in front of the class so she could keep her eye on me. Nonsense.

I just knew with being in the 8th grade, my last year. I had a load of school work. I was really getting tired of wearing those uniforms. Believe me. Dad was happy Mrs Smith was my teacher. Honestly, with the nine of us, we became an outfit. Ivy Wright was nothing to play with. No student in all my years knowing Ivy, no one crossed her. She'll check you in a minute. I believed she had a dream that she was "Dorothy" in the WIZ Musical. She and Angela became two "Sistas" that looked out for each other. Both of them, fully developed as young women. They all had the same taste in music and boys. Angela was attentive and becoming more attractive. David and Ivy were the tallest in our class. I was the next in line. Maurice and Chris was becoming more the best of friends. They were really got along. Derek Was still "Pickified", making silly jokes, drawing comic book pictures and me looking ridiculous. Lorena was coming along and slowly growing up but she was more quiet.

The friction between Miss Lugo and I reached to a boiling point. So, to start it off. Mrs Smith wanted me to go to her class and get some papers or that sort. I was getting angry. I walked to her class with a mean look on my face and asked her that Mrs Smith wanted some information. Miss Lugo was listening to me but I really didn't want to do this. She noticed that I had a hostile expression on face. And I quickly walked away. I returned to class and I made up something But Mrs Smith didn't quite understand. So, She made Angela go instead. I was tensed. Angela was upset with me and we had an exchange of words. "She doesn't know what's wrong with you." But I snapped back at her. OH MY GOODNESS! What's going on here??? So, about a few weeks after that. At school, on a Monday or Tuesday, still the beginning of the year. We had recess. We returned to class. We had our break to freshen up. Now, I wasn't in no mood this day. I was in the hallway, standing against the wall. Miss Lugo came walking down politely. As she walked passed me, I was making some noisy sounds to distract her. She stopped. She caught and stopped me. "I don't know what your problem is but you need to stop!!" She demanded. As she grabbed me just to control me. Nothing physical. I roared, "Get your Hands off of me!" That's all I Said. Ms Lugo looking very furious as she walked away. I had my arms folded. Eddie White walked up to me and said, "Travis, leave Ms Lugo alone, man." So the Drama began, Mrs Birdell Smith saw me and she slowly walked up to me. "What's going on between you and Ms Lugo?" I mumbled and I said, "I Hate Her!!!" So as we returned to class. I was still in the hall with Mrs Smith as she asked Ms Lugo to explained what happened. "I don't know what I did to Travis." She replied furiously, "When he was in my class, he would try to kiss my hands all over and that stuff!" Mrs Smith let me vent my anger, "You gave me a Conduct Referral, I didn't deserve!!" Mrs Smith, then told me to apologize to her directly. I fired back, "I'm sorry." Holly Barrett, who was in the 7th grade peeked out the door to see what was happening. There was murmurs in class. Mrs Smith made me returned to class. I sat down to my desk. With a Growling angry expression on my face. I wanted to go off and attack Angela as sat her in desk behind me. In some ways, she instigated it. I was quiet as an owl. I was in extreme rage. Manic Rage, I would admit. But class resumed.

SO LADIES AND GENTLEMEN. I RECEIVED MY FIFTH CONDUCT REFERRAL!! HOORAY!!!

Mrs Smith immediately got to business. So, I got home wasn't in trouble really. I think in it Mrs Smith wrote to imply that I was using profane language and threatened Miss Lugo. FALSE!! As I told you. Mrs Smith and Sr Saundra were there to protect Ms Lugo. I guess she wasn't a real true teacher to handle me. Yes, I was in trouble. Deep Trouble. Now, I was the Villain. "Travis, YOU ARE GULITY! FOR DISRESPECTING A TEACHER FOR YOUR FOUL LANGUAGE AND MISTREATMENT TOWARDS DENISE LUGO!" YOUR BEHAVIOR WILL NOT BE TOLERATED. DISCIPLINARY ACTION WILL BE TAKEN."

I was hardly spoken to by my classmates. Evidently, everybody was against me. It was like a Scandal. But I was extremely angry at that Fourth and Fifth Conduct Referrals. I was in serious Hot Water. I was suprised that Dad and my Family wasn't angry at me. My Father came to the Conclusion that I was always in trouble with it came to Ms Lugo and Mrs Smith. So joyful that this was my final year there. Maurice and Morgan were concerned too because when we were in 7th grade near the end of that year. Matt, Maurice, Morgan and I were on thin ice. Sr Saundra sent a letter to us about us on how we "Cuttin up" in Class. Well, Maurice warned me.

First, I was at Math Class, our New Pastor, Fr McHugh "WILDEYE" called me in and wanted me to come with him to his office. The Pastor's Office. This was no joke. I'm telling you. A bright sunny morning, I followed him as he had that Conduct Referral in his hand. Honestly, I was getting nervous. Fr McHugh was a short, stout and chubby man. With curly brown bushy neatly styled. He sported a bushy mustache. And it was only his second year as clergyman at the church. He had an eye infection in one of his eyes which he blinks constantly whenever he talks. He was nicknamed "WILDEYE". He smoked regularly but he was fond of me because since I was still an altar boy and he could rely on me. As, I entered his office, There was a table of papers and A Kitchen. Few Crucifixion crosses in various rooms and the den. And paintings of Christ. I was there in his office. "Sit down Travis." He said softly. A comfortable chair I sat down as he began to talk to me. That conference was more like I was on trial for committing the Crime of the Century. Like, Cpt Willard

Benjamin, from the film, "APOCALYPSE NOW", "This was the end of the river alright." He discussed with me on what happened with my altercation with Miss Lugo. He wanted to figure out what the problem with me was. But what shocked and struck him was that reason I said I hated her. Also, the issue was that was me. I answered and spoked softly but not too much. Alot was boiling in me. Which will be prevalent on me as the years to come. He looked serious but being broad minded and concerned because I was child of 14 for Goodness Sake. A pubescent preteen. He pointed out some of my issues about myself. The triumphant performance at the Christmas Musical performance the previous December. He never saw nothing like that before. Rightly so, I was on top of the world that night. Fr McHugh asked me if I had a crush on her. I responded yes. In some ways, I was lost with words. Again, I spoked softly and I told him that morning in his office, that I felt that some of the teachers at St Ann School were racists. To conclude in defending myself I told Fr McHugh, "I just want to live a simple clear life."

That day during recess, Sr Saundra and our new Pastor Fr McHugh "WILDEYE" approached to me that they wanted to speak to my parents. Maurice and Morgan were feeling anxious as they asked me what did Fr McHugh and I talked about. They were sensing about those letters Sr Saundra sent to them earlier that year. It was about my friction with Ms Lugo. In truth, I was still annoyed and bothered by that. When I got home later that day, I told my parents that they wanted to speak to them. My parents agreed and that they need to converse with the school about what took place. The next day afterschool, that evening, My parents and I came to his office. My Parents were greeted kindly and there was another with a TV and Fr McHugh walked me to another room with a Television. It was messy with papers everywhere. He gave me the remote control. He Said, jokingly, "Travis, if you say anything about my office being messy, I'm going bite your nose." So, My parents were in the den as I was when he spoke to me. At the end of conference, We went home. I came to the conclusion that I promised my parents not to get into anymore trouble. I continued not speaking to her for awhile. Continually, my classmates were against me.

Aside from that, I was finally getting the wish I granted. A St Ann's School Band. Our music instructor Mrs Sarah Frazier. A nice young lady. And she had a temper. She was short and stout built with her demeaning glasses with a broad mind of music. I liked her a lot. I really did. Auditions held in mid-October. I wanted to play the drums. Drums was my THING! And still is to this day. Listening to Prince Albums and the "777-9311" Beat countless times and many others. I wanted to be on the Band. I wanted to form a band with my classmates. I went to Edwards Music Store on McPherson Church Road. My father came along with me. I rented a snare drum and got a drum lesson book. And I got to it! In learning to play the drums, I was more comfortable in the traditional grip handling the sticks than the Matched Grip. When I was at the house, I was loud practising in the kitchen. I couldn't do in my room because My room was next to my parents. Our school Band was small but I was more dedicated. Our members were, Morgan Hardwick played the trumpet. He was pretty good at it. Matt Bradley played the Saxophone. Lia Shorter played the Clarinet and Amy Goodwin played the flute. Eddie White, Tiecel Mckoy of "THE FOUR HORSEMEN OF THE APOCALYPSE", Sarah Pollitt (Jill Pollitt's younger adorable sister) and the other girl whose last name was Lloyd. I forgot her name. There were a few students in our little band But I couldn't remember. I wanted us to be the Best.

I was so immersed in music I just became a Fanatic. I loved watching Movies on HBO, CINEMAX and SHOWTIME. Since, we had Cable Television but only a few in my neighborhood had cable. It was expensive and my Father could afford it. Carla and Craig Douglas had it. Hip Hop was emerging as ever. It was like everybody wanted to be a Rapper. RUN-DMC, Curtis Blow, The Fat Boys, Grandmaster Flash and the Furious Five. What struck me about this new fashion of music was the "Funky Beats". I would make beats in Class that drove Mrs Smith and my class up the wall. All of that was created in my head.

I did my best as a drummer for the St Ann's Band. Now, this was the period that I was very Hyper Manic, Moody and Irritable, indeed. But I clowned with the two members of, "THE FOUR HORSEMEN OF THE APOCALYPSE". Matt Bradley concentrated on his saxophone. Since, Mrs Sarah Frazier was my music teacher, we even talked about music. When, we had our practice Mrs Sarah Frazier. Actually, I was self taught on the drums. But I couldn't escape of my Drama with Ms Lugo. One Friday morning, at church we had Mass service. There was one song that all the class sung together. I didn't feel like singing at all. Sr Saundra saw me not singing,"Travis, You can sing it", She said to me to make me feel bad about what I did to Ms Lugo. After the Mass services, We returned to class, Morgan Said, "Sr Saundra got you Trav." I fired back at him, "I don't care". Even, Eddie approached me as he shook his head, "I Don't know. She embarrassed you." It was still a problem for me. Highly annoyed by that Episode. I was getting angry again. Sr Saundra, Mrs Smith and Fr "WILDEYE" McHugh was watching my every move.

Honestly, it was bothering me. After a few weeks, I was thinking just apologize to Ms Lugo just to get the heat off of me. I didn't want to but I had to do it. So, one Cloudy Day in October, in recess, I was wondering around with Angela Butler telling to me go to Ms Lugo's Class. "Just do it, Travis, Go on" She insisted. I was a little nervous. So, I slowly walked in her class and I said softly. As she looked at me, when she was having her lunch. I was being a Gentlemen. Her Face grew with such Joy and Happiness, I thought she was going to weep and cry. I could tell that it was bothering her. "I'm sorry", As I walked towards her. She put hand around me Like I said she was going to weep. I didn't realize that it hurt her terribly. Angela saw it and she highly aroused with great excitement. "I'm so proud of you. I could kiss you," Said Angela and she was getting a little emotional too. NO! I didn't want that.

I didn't feel better but as I said the HEAT was off of me. Mrs Smith was so proud that I apologized to Ms Lugo, she told me one morning in the Hall and she kissed me. Big Deal. I didn't really see it as a resolution with my friction with her but it was still the School worshipping Ms Lugo. From time to time, I would come to see her and chat with her afterschool. Angela Butler and a few kids too. Aside from that, I was concentrating on my Drums. Later that month, Halloween Night, there was a party that night and my Dad came with me. I was moody but I knew my Dad's ways. Maurice was there and he looked at me like, "You're going to get it." But Dad was in a good Spirits. The Halloween Party was held in the school and Social Hall. I felt mildly depressed for some reason that night. Ms Lugo and by SUPRISE her mother was there. She was so happy to speak with my Father about me. Dad was calm and content. There was music playing and Mrs Smith wanted to dance with me. I refused but she wanted me to enjoy myself all because my apology to Ms Lugo.

Still, I was in a playful mood and I tagged along with Maurice and Morgan, I think He was chasing Holly Barrett. A very cute attractive girl with her dirty brownish-blonde 80's new wave cut hair do and nice blue or hazel eyes in the 7th grade. She had a BIG CRUSH on Morgan. Towards the end of the Party Since our combined class, The Boys were looking at the Girls and checking them out. Eddie White was the true player. Believe me. Being a Class Clown, He had a way with the girls. Even at special occasions at school, like the picture days when we didn't have to wear our uniforms, He was very well dressed. He really matured by the time he reached the 7th grade with his deep voice. He was good in sports and he could dance.

As the Days at St Ann School went on and on, I put in alot of effort into my school work. I was being with our little School Band and It was my Heart and Soul. Mrs Frazier was very upset at times whenever we come late for class. I think that was a problem. The new sixth Grade teacher, Mrs Savage, who was pregnant was annoying at times. She had a cross eye. Pale white Skin with auburn hair. She had to be in her twenties. She was my Science Teacher. I remember Maurice made a funny joke about her having cross eyed. Mrs Smith taught Math with the 7th grade combined. Since the time, I reached the 6th grade, we had to exchange classes in the morning. The same with those Reading Groups But it was different this time.

Mrs Smith taught Three Reading courses which was the last class before dismissal from School.

Tonya was a senior at Reid Ross Sr High and it was learned Reid Ross was changed to be a Junior High by the Cumberland County schools and Fayetteville City Schools. It changed the district for Students in the Neighborhoods to attend different schools. Tonya told me that I will be Attending Terry Sanford Sr High. It was a controversial subject and it was even on broadcast local News. The Students of Reid Ross protested. She didn't agree with it either. During, this time Tonya applied to several Colleges that she wanted to attend. She got accepted to North Carolina State University in Raleigh.

As, Fall arrived, November arrived, I got really sick with a sore throat for a several days. My parents wanted me to attend school anyway. Even Chris Franklin was sick and I remember he was absent one day.

Mrs Frazier was planning a Christmas musical. I forgot the name of it. All nine of us didn't know the songs as rehearsals was taken place. The Kids who participated did a great Job. But, Morgan said, "Ours was better". There was a little kid in the 2nd and 3rd that sung a gentle song and he sounded good. I know the lyrics he sung, "Where can I Find him." The parents were proud of children performing the musical. My applause.

Christmas 1984 was a real good one. I got myself A DRUM SET. It was red with a snare, Tom and Bass with one cymbal. And I got a FISHER Big Stereo Box System with a Double Cassette Player. And I got clothes too. Teasie was still with and Dante' was nine months old and we got a lot of presents. I got my little Drum set and got to it. I played them too hard and we took my set to our barely standing Barn in our backyard.

Now, I have small drum set. I felt that I was the King of the World. Well, not much a King. I was enjoying in doing something that uplifted my self-esteem. Simultaneously, I felt that I can achieve anything.

The neighbors heard my loud drumming. No, I didn't feel like I was a Celebrity. But the characters of THE BOTTOM knew that I was getting down on the drums.

My new FISHER Stereo Box and I had a few Prince cassette tapes and I played them since it was the holidays. I kept my volume low and I listened to them. I was hungry for all kinds of music. We had another new Black radio Station in Fayetteville. Foxy 99.1. It was the rise of Hip Hop.

January 1985. A New Year But a real cold one. At School, there was an accident in our Classroom. The Pipes to our Heater Bursted in our Classroom and it formed Ice. A Huge Chunk and the Floor was Very Wet. Watered down. The Classroom was in Bad Shape. Mrs Smith was furious about it. It took about a week for the pipes to be fixed and repaired by the Plumber. And School resumed.

February, Mrs Frazier planned a field trip for to visit a recording studio on McPherson Church Road. It was for both Classes. The 7th were acting like Clowns and they couldn't go with us. It was just only the nine of us that went. Morgan Hardwick knew the guys out there and they gave us a tour of the place. But guess who was the center of attention??? I was everywhere. My classmates cheered for me as I went to test the microphone in he soundroom. There were instruments there and along with was a Full Drum Set and I got to it. And I just played and no one can stop me. I played using the Matched Grip holding my sticks. Mrs Frazier sensed This, "He's highly talented on the DRUMS". So the rest of the eight came to me and I played, "I Feel For You" by Chaka Khan with Grandmaster Mellie Mel. Written By Prince. A real Funky Jam with a Funky Beat. And then what really topped it off, Angela, Ivy and Morgan, HELL all of them rapped to "Roxanne Roxanne" By UTFO. I knew the Beat and played along with them. So, the Guys in the Studio recorded me playing the Drums and TO THIS DAY I HAVE IT ON CASSETTE. Everybody rooted for me. To conclude this, I was rising but it was not to be so.

Spring. March-May 1985. Alot of things were taken place at the little parochial school on 365 N Cool Spring Street. Everything was going so fast for me during my last year.

Mrs Frazier approached to me and she was BLOWN AWAY!! She told me that I was so talented and what made it so Great that she wrote a message letter to my Family that She suggested that I should get a Private Drum instructor. That Day, My Father came Home from Work. Walked through the door and I gave Dad the paper I'll never forget what he did. He looked at it and placed on our wooden cabinet in our den. He walked to the kitchen. I don't know what he did with it.

I can't explain what was in that man's Head. I was too afraid to ask him and I never did. Dad was just a Working man. Don't Question Dad. Enough Said.

I needed to get my Bass Foot pedal fixed to drum set. Yes, My Father and I went to Edwards Music, And we talked with one of the salesman and he said that it would cost $350 to fix my Bass Foot Pedal. And my Dad turned around asked me "Do you have $350? I answered softly, "No". Again, Enough Said.

Mrs Frazier really wanted me to continue playing the drums. Unfortunately, It never meant to be. There was an event something like a talent show. I was absolutely chosen to perform my drums at the social hall. Everyone in my class me. Yet, I was hurt. Eddie White and I argued concerning it. So, I went to Secretary Mrs Chaffin as she was typing the Program with and I told her that I won't be performing. I felt real miserable that I let my classmates down real Horrorshow.... Ruefully, I let myself down.

There was so much expectations for me. Mrs Frazier was very disappointed and upset and she hardly talked to me at that time. Again, there I suffering from mild depression. I did all that Boasting and Bragging that I was perform my Drums for my classmates of my School. Drums was my passion and It was my love. I knew I could accomplished so much If I continued.

As for our Band, we had to perform during the Spring Musical. I forgot some of the pieces that we done. We rehearsed and we did the Best that we could. I had a real hard time reading music to the Drums. Now the First Instruction Book was fairly easy. But it was just only for snare drum. For example, the basic rudiments and the notes which I found was frustrating. I felt that I didn't need to read music but Years Later I would know the Importance of Music Theory.

Then the Time of Easter arrived, we had a short play about the Passion of Christ. I was chosen to play the disciple, Peter. Matt Bradley, Ayana (who was in THE GREAT LATE POTENTATE musical), She was very good. Andy Shepard (Lorena's younger brother) was chosen to play Christ. He was to wear a big white robe. Have his arms spread out with a brown card shaped like a cross with a rope tied around him. To create the crucifixion. I had only a Few lines to say. Holly Barrett and Angela were the narrators. Mrs Smith wanted us really to be in our characters. Now, when it came to me, when Christ was Arrested and convicted of claiming he was equivalent to God. And my part was the Denial of Peter where I say the main line, "I do not know the Man!" a few times. I didn't yell. I had to express the anger and fear as Peter was denying his Lord. As the people in Jerusalem accused him of being a disciple of Christ. He was in such trauma and depression. I had to wear a costume I found at the house, it was Tonya's purple house coat or whatever it was. I remember, Kowalski Plummer and Tiecel McKoy was teasing about what I wore. THE FOUR HORSEMEN OF THE APOCALYPSE was back. Instead of Calling me, "Musky", They would call me "Morris Lump" because the Shape of my head and my high admiration for Morris Day and the TIME.

Then there was Sex Education. It was really ridiculous. We already knew about it. Enough Said. Boys were Boys. Girls were Girls. But I knew one thing; Ivy Wright was getting tired of St Ann School. "I'm tired of all these girls around here. I can't wait to get the hell outta here," she said eagerly.

Bazzar- May 1985. I went there, most of the gang were there. I was all out. My Behavior, I must say. I was antsy because I didn't want to do the USA FOR AFRICA. It was the song Mrs Smith wanted us to sing "We Are The World" for our performance. She definitely wanted me to participate in it. My opinion, The song was good but not great. It was all the latest music artists performing to raise money for the Hunger and Poverty in Africa. Since I was the only eighth grader to sing the song with a few 7th graders. We rehearsed it the week before. But everybody was actually looking up to me. Why?? Because my voice was slowly changing. It wasn't high enough anymore when we did our Christmas Musical Back in '83. Yes, we knew the lyrics to the Song. It wasn't hard really. I was picked to do the Bruce Springsteen chorus. Tiecel sung the Stevie Wonder part. I remember when it came to me singing as the rehearsal was taking place in class. "Sing it through your heart, Travis", Mrs Smith said encouragingly. Maurice Thomas was supposed to sing but he didn't want to be part of it. So, that day, I was getting ready BUT! They already performed it. I didn't understand that. Eddie White told me we already did it. To this Day, It baffles me to think about it. We were getting closer to Graduation. Yes, all nine of us were excited and ready to attend new schools. We slowly was cleaning out our desks. I injured my middle finger as I was throwing away the papers. I clumsy threw the paper to our Gray trash Bucket and my Hand struck the edge of bucket which caused me to injure my middle finger as it quickly swollen for a couple of days. Class was still in session. 5th grade-8th grade went to a Trip to the Cape Fear River, it was Cloudy that day and a little chilly that Friday during the last week of May. We went on this tour and we were all on this boat rowing on the river. It was a long day. Morgan Hardwick and I had our stereo Boxes blaring, RUN-DMC, Klymaxx, Prince and the Revolution and Jesse Johnson. Rehearsals for the Graduation also took place. We could all do what we want. It was all Fun though.

June-1985. It was all nine of us to decide what activities we wanted to do as the Graduating Class. We had a Breakfast Brunch as you know I ate like a hog that was held in the Library and we also had a Conference with Fr McHugh "WILDEYE" at the church and that morning we acted DAMN CLOWNS. Mrs Smith caught us "Red Handed", She got Highly Furious! We were playing around in the Lord's House. Now, we still had to wear our uniforms. We decided to Go to White Lake in Bladen County that First Saturday of June. Not all of us went to the lake that Morning, Just the six of us. Angela, Ivy, Lorena, Chris, Derek and I. It was sort of boring. Going to a Lake would have been much Fun if All nine of us were there. Mrs Smith and Ivy's Mother came with us. I rode with Angela and her mother. This I must say, While, I was riding with those two young Ladies, they talk SO MUCH ALIKE! Also, Angela's Grandmother!! Chris, Derek and I went to the arcade. It had a few video games. But the one which was popular was this game Called, COBRA COMMAND. It was an awesome game. The Objective was to eliminate terrorists in the US. And The US Army was to accomplish the mission by being on a Heavily Equipped Helicopters. Derek and Chris wanted me out of the Way because they wanted to some other things. The Girls were wearing Bathing suits. Lorena wore a Bikini But Angela was looking really curvy. She wore a Royal Blue Bathing Suit and I forgot what Ivy wore. Mrs Smith injured herself on leg or foot. It wasn't serious though. But, it was getting hot that Day. We wasn't there too long. Ivy and Morgan threw parties at their houses several days after.

Sunday, June 2nd, 1985-Graduation.

It Finally came....It Finally came.

The Commencement for the St Ann School Class of 1985 was held at the St Ann Catholic Church.

To be honest, I couldn't believe it. My eight years of attending that little school at 365 N Cool Spring Street came to a cessation. I was wearing a gray suit with a light blue shirt and a red tie. No, I didn't have Baggies. That's what I really wanted. My Family came with me. I was feeling proud. I went into the School and I was met with a big suprise, THE FOUR HORSEMEN OF THE APOCALYPSE were dressed Sharp! They tried to the "Chilli Sauce" from the TIME as we clowned. The 7th grade hosted our graduation as we did the previous year. Eddie White was looking handsome in his Suit. As we prepared for the ceremony. We took photos of each other. I was looking proud. Angela was wore this Big White Gown as if she was getting married. She Complemented me on how looked in my suit. I did the same for her. The 7th Grade hosted our graduation. So, we walked to the Church and we all nine of us Assembled. The "Pomp and Circumstance" composed by Sir Edward Elgar was played on an Organ by one of the "Den Mothers". Our parents looked exultant as Angela Butler, Chris Franklin, Morgan Hardwick, David Lee, Derek Sellers, Lorena Shepard, Maurice Thomas, Ivy Wright and I slowly walked to the front of the Church altar. Fr "WILDEYE" McHugh performed the services. But the life of the graduation was Morgan's little sisters. His Mother trying to keep her kids in check. Everybody laughed at them. I was quiet and attentive. But I was really thinking inside. What's next? As, Sr Saundra announced our Full names to receive our diplomas. We also gave Flowers to our Mothers. At the end of the service, Fr "WILDEYE" McHugh approached gave me a Big huge Smile and firm Handshake. I Was feeling Proud with a Big Smile. So, Refreshments was served At the Social Hall. And of course, I was Manic, But I noticed that Eddie and a few others was sort of like giving me the cold Shoulder. "You better stop Acting like that in High School." He warned me. All that I knew I was fully new Alumni of St Ann Catholic School.

The Next day, Monday morning. I went to school. I think it was the last day of school. I walked down the Hall and much to my suprise, my Fellow Alumni was there. They were in the Library and just socializing. "I wish you could've went off on Miss Lugo", said Ivy. "I wish you could've slap her down!" As you know Ivy Wright was nothing to play with really. She was so excited that she graduated from St Ann School. Then, we all planned to go to Biscuit Kitchen to have lunch. We walked in a single file line because the school had fence around it. It wasn't a long walk But we got there and we hung out. We were kids.

June 16, 1985. My Birthday. I entered my fifteenth year on this earth. I went with my mother and Tonya Shopping at the Cross Creek Mall. Partly, it had to do with Tonya getting ready for College. Mom gave me some money and I treated myself. I went to Record Bar and I purchased a cassette tape, 'The Essential Jimi Hendrix' and paperback book, "The Godfather" By Mario Puzo. As we were going to various shops at the Mall, I started reading it immediately. I fried my Brain in the Book but earlier that spring, I bought Puzo's latest Book, "The Sicilian" It was hard to read at first but within time I loved it. Mario Puzo is one my favorite Authors. I was so fascinated about organized Crime and how that "Life" the mobsters lived. It always fascinated me. Also, the Itailian and Sicilian Culture meant alot to me too. The beauty of Italy and Sicily. Since, I am Catholic I know that religion is very important to the native Sicilians and

Italians. But I keep promising myself that I will Travel to Sicily. I will before I leave this Earth.

The movie "The GodFather and The Godfather PART II" were perhaps one of the greatest Films ever made. I loved every character. It's one of those Films that you never never get tired of watching. You're immediately drawn to it. Now, there are Websites on Social Media everywhere. You know the lines and quotes. It's a popular culture now.

I Loved Jimi Hendrix. I remember Morgan talking about the WOOSTOCK FESTIVAL and Hendrix's Historic performance of "THE STAR SPANGLED BANNER". As I many times I've listened to it and watched on TV, Video and my DVD set of his show, the sound effects still kills me to this day How that Man displayed it on his White Fender Stratocaster, Expressing and pointing out what was Happening in the turbulent 60's in America. A young Man who expired at 27 was a flame burning on a candle but it was blown away and gone forever.

Late June. It was time for Tonya to go to Raleigh and move in her dorm to start her college studies. Mom, Dad and I said our farewells. Yes, I didn't want her to go. Teasie left early February to go Omaha, Nebraska with her new born son and stayed with her In-Laws. Then it was just me at 734 Eufaula Street. This was going to be difficult period for me.

Since, it was time for me to get ready for me to attend a new School. St Ann School was History. I had to attend Hillcrest Junior High on 590 Winding Creek Road. My Father and I went there to register and Mr Lawson was the Principal. I was more concerned about joining the School Band but I couldn't. There was already auditions. So, that was out. I was sort of lost because I didn't know about the Classes I took, Typing and Industrial Arts. I just did it.

Well, At THE BOTTOM, all the kids that were my age attended Hillcrest. I was worried about it. Though, Carla Douglas, my next door neighbor was already a student she knew about the school and she talked to me about it and she showed me her latest Yearbook. So, I tagged along with her.

FLY GIRL by the Boogie Boys was the big song in the Hip Hop Music scene that Summer. Craig, Carla's Brother had a new white Car and he was Blasting that song out! We hung out around the town.

As of course, Carla was telling me about Hillcrest about a few of her classmates. Still, it was a worry for me. I was becoming a little more Depressed. Getting ready to go to another School. I really missed my former Classmates. As for the Gang at St Ann School, Mrs Smith was more concerned about me than all the nine of us. First, she suggested that I should take General Math. And secondly, she talked with my father about me. I was lonely and everyone in my Family was gone.

September 1985 – February 1996

This was the period that my symptoms of Bipolar Type I was in Full Swing. The most difficult, traumatic and agonizing stage which I was declining. Persecuted for being, "different". Rejected. Making a "Fool" out myself. Periods of Grief and Dealing with Stigma by the kids. My Friendships with the"Gang" will be tested. Betrayal. Being SHUT OUT. My Family becoming concerned about me and my behavior as I was Fighting and arguing with them. "Pains of Growing up" All those traits brought me down. And I had no one. To the time I attended Winston-Salem State University, I Needed Help. I did it on my own.

"I've journeyed cross the desert sands through raging storms and robber Bands. I sought this place long after the Star had disappeared."

My Aunt Bronnie threw a Family Get together at her house on Labor Day. It was just a regular day but it was very Hot day. The Food was good as always. My cousins Natasha and her siblings were there enjoying themselves with their new Family pool. My cousin Flamont had a Girlfriend and he was in the Military. He was Feeling good and making everybody feel good in the Family. But, I was just me. When we returned home. I was tired. Took a Bath. Went to bed early that night. I had to get prepared for my First Day in School.

Tuesday, September 3, 1985. I got up. And I got dressed. Before my parents left for Work they gave me $1.00 and a key to the house when I return home. I wore a Knit Red Maroon Shirt, New Blue Levi Jeans, I wore snow White socks and Nike Sport Shoes. I took with me my pencil and a thin blue note book. I went to my parent's bathroom and I looked at myself in the mirror. It was going to be a long Day. I came out of the house. I walked up to the Eufaula St sign and I joined Carla Douglas and Cindy Gershon. It was a cool day but It got intensely Hot. They chatted about school and where I need to go when we arrive at the school. So, the School Bus No.721 came and it stopped. There were lots of Kids on that Bus. I thought to myself, "Fuck". I slowly got on the Bus. There were Kids. Street Kids with mean nasty expressions on their Faces and they all looked at me. "Look at the Shoes". Now I couldn't find a seat. Still, I walked slowly and I saw this Black boy sitting all By himself and I said softly, "Can I sit here?" He looked at me and moved over and I sit. "Damn, He told you to move the Fuck outta the Way!", said one Kid And all the Kids Laughed. So the Bus drove off to Hillcrest Jr High. Then all the kids were talking and cracking jokes. Never have I heard so much Profanity from those Kids mouths on the Bus that morning and it will continue for the rest of my 3 and □ years in Public School and Life in General. I was sitting in my seat and as the bus drove I looked through the Window as Buildings was passing by I was going to a New School.

As the bus finally arrived at Hillcrest Jr High. I got off the Bus. I Called myself 'William' instead of Travis. Don't Know Why I did that just so I think it would be cool to be Called "William'. I'm the Same Person.

I went to the student hall. It was dark and a few lights. There were lots of students. I knew I couldn't find where sit. As I sat there on those Big Steps. Somehow, out of the Blue, My name was Called and I started the Shit. The Manic Behavior. So, I walked slowly to a room with lots of students. It was home room and my home room Teacher was Mrs McLewis. A very nice Lady. I was given my classes I had registered. My Classes were English I, P.E., Home room, Typing, Government Civics, Physical Science, General Math and Industrial Arts.

And I must say that Day and as School continued, I hardly did my homework. I was in my Own World. The Students. All of Them knew I was naive, introverted and would do anything to get a laugh. Most of my classes that I had were African-American. I must say

Thugs. They were Street Smart. They already figured me out. None of them liked me.

But I must say that there's one name that I was called all those 3 and □ Years. A name that I detest to this day, "CRAZY". I hated that name. Comparatively, I rank it as being called a "NIGGER". I was called worse names than that. It's not an exaggeration. This is no joke. On "How I act in High School" is one of their catch phrases. Being bullied by Sadistic Fucks who has no life for themselves. As for me, "Only the Strong can survive". I will also say that there was Racism, of course. The High society White Students that lived on Raeford Road, Van Story Hills, Haymount, McPherson Church Road. The Southern Belles. "Fine White Girls". But there were frictions between the White Students "Preps" and the "Hippie Crew", They were the most down to Earth. So, Terry Sanford High was a Thug-Prep School. I Hated The School. I Hated the School. I Hated the School. I Hated the School. I Hated the School. I Hated the School. I Hated the School.

As that turbulent, Traumatic time for me in my life. My Body was going through serious changes. My voice was still high-pitched. Since, I was so Manic, I didn't care but it didn't bother me.

Carla and Cindy were always talking about those Kids on our Bus in the morning. Negative Children whose behavior was worse than mine. I was more concerned about being Accepted rather concentrating on my School Work. I would do anything for a Laugh. But I was making a Fool of myself. As my " Post St Ann School Years" were going on. I would always say to myself, "Getting used to the System". It didn't make any sense at all. Yes, I made "Associates" there at Hillcrest Junior High and Terry Sanford High. After all, I did made a few friends But most of them turned on me Because of "How I acted". That wasn't being, "Popular". Some of the Students I socialized with had in common. Music, for one thing. My Silliness highly offended the Girls. The black girls. That's right. I said it!! Never have I knew of Black Girls with the "Crabbiest Attitudes and Filthy Mouths". Yes, there were few who liked me but I couldn't behave myself. That's the truth. Carla Douglas tried to fix me up with a girl named Amanda Hanes. She really did liked me. I started out fine but hanging out with those fools. I hurt her feelings and bothers me to this day, thinking about her. I was teased like, "You ain't had no pussy?" "You scared of Pussy?" "Mother Fucker scared of pussy". "You like titties?, You know Breasts". "Will's retarded ass messin everything up."

I listened to Jimi Hendrix. I loved the Man. I loved the MAN!!! BUT HE DIED SO FUCKING YOUNG!! I acted in class like I can a play an electric guitar. Feel like him! Be like Him!!! Hearing the Records with the Jimi Hendrix Experience! Are you experience?? Yes, I am experienced. I wish that I was at the Woodstock Festival!! I'm Jimi Hendrix flying through a great Blue Sky and Kissed the Sky.

"You think you can play a guitar?? You're Crazy! CRAZY!!! He's CRAZZZIIIEE!, the kids would say. Who's this Boy? He Stupid and Crazy! CRAZY HORSE! HEY GIRL, HE CRAZY! TALKIN TO HIMSELF! YOU BE ACTIN DUMB IN CLASS. STOP ACTING CRAZY. NEVER HAD NO PUSSY! YOU KNOW WHAT PUSSY IS??? ARE YOU A VIRGIN? WASSUP, KILLAH?? "FUNNY SHAPE HEAD" HE WALK SO FUNNY!" I watched "Police Academy" and I like Michael Winslow's Vocal Effects making Machine Gun Noises. So I made my Own Machine Gun Noises in Class. Disturbing and Disrespecting the Teachers as he or she was conducting class.

Carla, What's wrong with your friend, William? He's acts Stupid! I can't Stand Him! "Well, At least he tried to talk to you," She objected. She defended for me. People are Talking about you. They're saying YOU CRAZY! Crazy Mother Fucker!! Crazy Ass! Just Crazy! It reached to the point I had to defend myself at times and I knew some of the big guys I couldn't fight But you have to talk your junk and stand up to that person. Crack a few Jokes and then they'll leave you alone. Sometimes, you have to stand your ground. BUT HE DIDN'T HAVE ANY PUSSY.

Going to class, I hear names calling at me. But in P.E. Class, there was a few kids that I got to know. Now I wasn't acting. I was mostly quiet. Boris Yates, who lived in Evans Hill. I just approached him on the benches and I said, "My name is William McLaurin, Can we be friends? And I extended my hand. "He said, "Yeah man." He shook my hand in return. All of the Kids at Hillcrest Jr High. Boris was a young delightful handsome kid. Skinny but muscular, he was athletic when it came to Basketball. He had light brown eyes and a pleasant smile. He knew everybody at that school and everybody knew him. He was sneaky though. But he was "untouchable". He could crack jokes on you. And he had own circle friends. Few of them I could get along. Then there was riding the bus that I had to deal with. The kids were loud talkative. Lastly, there were fights on the bus and on the school campus.

I was a well known "Perv" at times. Bothering and pulling innocent pranks on girls. I like Girls. Like I said, I'll do anything for a laugh. Sometimes the girls would tell me to behave myself. I wouldn't listen I'd just go on and do obnoxious shit which would piss some of the guys off. All the Boys would do it. Then you have to "JOCKS", who played Football and Basketball. They had girlfriends or girls who were crazy about them. "Being popular" was my objective and at the same time I wasn't paying attention in Class. The same thing that I was doing when I first attended 1st grade with Sr Janice. And I wasn't even doing my School work. It has been said, "If you don't learn from your past. You're doomed to repeat it."

Carla just couldn't really talk to me at times. And my sister Tonya would receive letters from her telling me about behavior and what I was doing but she could figure out the reason. I would be nasty to her. Towards the end when I attended Terry Sanford She wouldn't even talk to me. Boris Yates sometimes would talk to me. But he had his Boys. He was starting a Club of his own called, 'The Happy Cat Club'. I was the first fool to join because we both had our lockers next to each other.

Tonya would come home and try to talk to me about myself but I just wouldn't listen. I was much too busy listening to Hendrix and many artists in Hip Hop. "The Show" "Lodi Dodi" By Slick Rick and Doug E Fresh. And of course, there were Fights at School and I was almost in one. I couldn't fight. Not really. I would usually punk

out. Since, I was an overly sensitive kid and I couldn't defend myself
I had to punk out. But I had my crushes on the Girls and yeah they
were HOT! They didn't like me. Because the "WAY I ACTED".
"PUSSY EATER '85!" Yeah. HOO HOO HOO HA HA HA!!

As, Fall of 1985 was falling in. The weather was entering to
Indian summer. Hillcrest Jr played Football against Reid Ross in
October. That all of a sudden, there was my "Gang", Angela, Ivy,
David, Derek and Maurice. We were still a close knit. They watching
the game on the bleachers. But Angela Butler was somewhat having
this attitude towards me. I knew that I made a joke about her but
she displaying this arrogant attitude about herself. I know that her
skin disorder was faded away and she becoming an attractive girl
but I guess she didn't have time for my "Silliness" or Hyper Mania
anymore. As She walked away from away with her new Friend. Not a
Guy yet. So, Maurice and I stuck together and we hung out. Maurice
and I walked around the football field and then I introduced him to
Boris Yates. That was a controversial call because one of the team
players of Hillcrest "Face Mask" during a play and we lost. Our
coach, Mr Brewington was furious as well. I heard that he called him
and blamed him for the lost. That was the talk of the school.

During that time, I got my School Pictures taken. It was going
to be on the school yearbook, 1985-86. I hardly smiled and didn't
even care. Then, Report cards came in November. Bad Grades. All
(E's). General Math and P.E. were better but I caught the Hell when
I returned home. Dad and Mom were arguing of course and this was
the Beginning of the Arguing and Fighting with my Parents.

Yes, I felt like I was in a prison with my parents. Very discouraged
about my Grades. My sisters were gone and living their own lives.
But slower and slower, I was going down. I knew that St Ann's was
over. I kept in touch with Vincent Robinson and Maurice Thomas.
I felt much better calling them. Especially Maurice But I still kept in
touch with all the gang. Sadly, It would reached to the point that I
had to let them go. Actually, I was still suffering about not continuing
with my deep passion for the Drums. DAMN IT. I couldn't be in
the Band and it just tore me apart. I am somebody. I Am the GIFT.

Christmas Holidays – 1985. Well, Since this was going to be a Different celebration of the First Coming of the Christ, There was a dance Held at the School. Yeah, I was there along some of the other guys who came late. They played all the latest in Hip-Hop and Pop Music. I wanted to feel like that I was life of the Party. I wore my occasional customary Blue Levi Jeans and the jacket and a long sleeve shirt with a my new red penny loafers. I was so excited to be there but most of the kids didn't want to see me. Because they knew I was going to make an "ASS' out of myself. Carla Douglas was there trying her best to make me feel welcomed by classmates who thought they we were a "Couple" but we were not. A few of the Kids enjoyed my company but without me making "Machine Gun" sounds. Trying to act like "Jimi Hendrix putting a red paper ribbon wrapped around my head. Clowning around. That dance was on a Thursday but the next day, I was the talk out of the school about how much of a "CRAZY ASS" that I was. OH, I hated being called that.

I started hanging around Boris Yates and his friends. They didn't want me around. FUCK IT. But there were parties that I was invited But I never attended. A Christmas musical at St Ann School was held. I went there and everyone was glad to see me again. I mean overly excited to see me. Especially, Eddie White. I guess they were thinking that I doing good in school But in truth I wasn't. Terrible Grades and having a difficult adjusting to Hillcrest. I couldn't tell them that. Eddie White was in the eighth grade and He was playing his snare drums for a musical. I have to say, he was performing very good. What was more painful was that I wasn't playing my drums anymore and the Damn Bass Foot Pedal was broken. I could do it! I could do it! I knew I could!! He was glad that he was leaving St Ann School the next year just as I did earlier in June.

Christmas 1985. It really wasn't a good Christmas. Tonya came home. All that we got was a General Electronics VCR. Tonya and I got a lot of clothes. Teasie was still in Omaha, Nebraska with her In-Laws and her son Dante' who just turned one years old. I was off the rack and I was glad that School was on Winter Break. Two Weeks and I can get some Sleep. I Hate Hillcrest Jr High. I hated that DAMN School. I was feeling distressed returning to the same 'ol Bullshit. Mean, Sadistic Negative Kids From the "Court". Let's Face it, I had no motivation for public school. Still acting like a Fool and scared to say "NO" when some of the kids sucker me out of my lunch money. They knew that I never attended public school before. I was the Kid, who went to that, "School" out there. Some of the Kids knew some my former fellow Classmates from St Ann's.

In highschool, as you know, being popular is the trend. Your appearance, the way you dress and your reputation. Standing up to yourself. Speak for yourself. Crack jokes and you get respect. Especially, if you're on the Bus. Me? Making a Fool out of myself. Really, I had no one to lean on. Carla Douglas did try to reach out to me.

February 1986 – Hillcrest Jr High gave the Skills Functional Exams. It tests your ability to Basic Reading and Mathematical Skills. And my friends, I never took that test seriously. I was just daydreaming at my homeroom. I had no motivation. A week or later. I got my scores. Low, very low. I guess I was one of the students who scored the lowest. Boris Yates scored very high and he wanted to see my score. I was a little irritable about it and depressed. "Will, why your score is so low, Man?' "This isn't no joke, Man." Humiliated I snatched the paper out of his hand. It was the end of the school day and I had to ride the bus. Then, when I got on the Bus and Amanda Hanes, she tried to talk to me. I couldn't even say a word to her because I was so ashamed of myself. She sensed it already. My grades were just horrible. I got home and I never gave the papers to my parents. I threw them away in my room. I needed Help, everyone.

I was going through my puberty phase and it was painful. My voice was changing as Misty noticed one evening as she called me so suprisingly. She was asking me about Morgan Hardwick. They both dated. Yes, the St. Ann's crew was still there and we kept in touch too. I was still thinking about Lori Hoskins from time to time. Plaintively, I knew she had forgotten about me.

Spring-1986. Spring came and what a time it was. Me, with bad failing Grades. Acting a Fool and having students dislike and doing things for a joke. Sick, tired and irritable of having to go to Raleigh to see Tonya for what??? I didn't want to go there on Sundays. It was a little hint of me not getting enough sleep. Rambling to myself. Just feeling real terrible. Roaring at my parents and close to getting physically "beat down" by my father. WHERE ARE YOU???? TRAVIS, WHERE ARE YOU???

I didn't know what I was thinking about. It was getting close to the end of the year. I already Failed English as my teacher once yelled at me. My parents were very concerned about me. From Mrs McLewis' suggestion that I should get evaluated. Speak to a Child Psychologist. That's what they did. Dr Spoleten was a chubby man with thick dark Brown hair. Very intelligent. I guess he knew me right off the bat. I was feeling like I was the villain But I just really couldn't express my true feelings. Mom and Dad were very concerned about me which was no problem. I don't think that Dr Spoleten never actually sensed my Behavior. HEY! I was just 15 and having a difficult time adjusting to a New School.

The third Nine Weeks- Report Cards. Same thing all (E's). This time My Father was furious. Not Talking to me. Giving me lectures. "Don't give me this Bullshit saying you're going to pass. You ain't gon' pass!!!!". I hated My Father helping me with Homework even when I was in St Ann's. I hated it. Because Half of the Shit was all wrong. I remember that I went to the grocery store with him. He met this lady who was a family friend to his family. And knowing my father was very upset of course. He talked and played his role socializing with her a few minutes. After she left, He went on to tell me, "Now you feel like shit about that report card!". That April, Teasie returns Home from Florida with John and Dante' just turned 2. As soon as they came home, My Dad argued terribly telling my sister my grades were horrible and I wasn't going to pass. He was at his Best that Night. Dad made me very angry but you can't do that at the McLaurin household of 734 Eufaula Street. To the last minute, I was trying to work hard to improve my grades. My mother was arguing with me. Screaming and yelling one morning Before I walked out of

the House about my Grades and she received a note from the School
that I was in danger of failing the 9th grade.

June 1986. The students were excited that school was over.
Summer was coming and I will be attending Terry Sanford Sr
High School. Some of the kids were like playing tricks and pranks.
One morning at school, Boris Yates and his "Happy Cat", crew
cheered,"TASTES GREAT!" And across the school building where
the preps hanged out shouted back, "LESS FILLING!" It was the
catch phrase from the, "Miller Light" beer commercial. There was
also a plan of having a "Food Fight". But it never happened. So,
to make this short, I barely passed some of my classes. A Few of
them I failed but I had to attend Summer School. I had to retake
Social Civics at Douglas Byrd, (June 1986-August 1986). A waste
of summer. After all that time, I wasted the regular School year not
concentrating on my Work as one Teacher preached you wouldn't be
here. So, I took Social Civics and passed it with a high "B". But my
Summer was Short. Tonya came home from College and We traveled
to Jacksonville, FLA. That My sister's Husband John was stationed
at for one week. We've been to Florida before during June '84.

When we returned home, Dad was pissed. Just pissed. So, later
that month my mother, Tonya and I went to Cross Creek Mall and
was shopping for new clothes for me School. There was a nice bright
yellow jacket and it was very expensive. It was DOPE! I'm telling you,
I really Liked that Jacket. But inside of myself, I was feeling nervous
and depressed. But when I registered for classes for the 10th grade.
I wanted to take Acting I and Art I as well as the required classes.

Sept 1986-June 1989. I attended Terry Sanford Sr High. Located
on 2301 Fort Bragg Road near Bragg Blvd. It was a very afflicting
and traumatic experience. After I graduated, I was emotionally and
mentally damaged. I would wake up in the around 6am. My mother
was always the first up in the house. She would make breakfast for
me. I would dress up and get my books, watch a little TV, The Disney
Channel. And it was time for me to catch the bus with Carla Douglas
and hop on the Damn Bus. The number for that particular bus was
No. 23.

Since, I was a Sophomore. It didn't take time for me to adjust to it. I just turned 16, the previous June. I was trying to make the best of it. I hated that School more so than I hated Hillcrest Jr high. But I must remember that I was attending a school with kids who were much older than me. 17-18 years old. But the Sophomores were looked upon as Rookies. I didn't kiss nobody's ass. There was Nothing about that school I liked.

Well, as my school work goes, my grades improved very much. But my Behavior was conspicuous. I was more attentive. Yet, the drama on the bus was mostly tensed among kids in the neighborhood. Fights would break out amid the boys and girls. Real stupid shit. There were some kids there that were friendly, I must admit to that. Now to be honest, it wasn't like my behavior was WILD and HORRENDOUS. It was from time to time.

One Sunday in October, at home we were having Breakfast and I noticed my voice was really changing. It felt like I had a Frog lounged down my throat. I felt it. Tonya came to the kitchen and she said, "Your voice is changing." Furthermore, I was experiencing "Wet Dreams" in my bed whenever I think about the girls I wanted to be with. But it never happened.

My awkward appearance chased the Kids away. Boris Yates had a new name for me, "CHRONIC HALATOSIS", as he and his friends turned on me. To them it was funny on the Bus. And that Yellow Jacket my Mother bought for was stolen. It was to the point I HATED MYSELF. I was called "Ugly" by the "Sistas". I was always mentioned by that name. And of course, "CRAZY" HAHAHA! My second Year in Public School and it was very very Terrible. I must admit to you, my Friends. I grieved.

There's so much that I can share in my book practically my adjusting to life during my "Post St Ann School Years". But I kept on crawling on those "Desert Storms and Robber Bands". But there is one incident that I must share with you. It occurred in January 1987, during Drama Class. My Drama teacher, Mrs Brandi, a nice pleasant woman was planning and starting a play, I forgot what it was called. It was on a Friday Afternoon and everyone knew about me. We were doing rehearsing on stage and I was experiencing an agonizing Sinus Headache. I was known for bothering and harassing the girls. But there was one girl I can't mention her name was bothering me. Now, I wasn't on the stage, I was sitting on one the chairs but I got up all of a sudden, And this girl was bothering me too, "Why don't you leave her alone??" I was annoying this girl in class. I admit to that. The Headache was really really bothering me. I was walking back and forth. Another girl named "Suzy" was asking me, "William, what's wrong?" I answered her softly, "I have a headache." But the other girl kept on and on. Telling me to "Leave her alone." And in Full Rage, I Grabbed a Book and hurled it at her. It didn't hit her at all. But the Class was shocked and it was quiet as a church. They looked all tensed and having fear of me. My classmates had their jaws dropped. They looked at me and at each other. My friends, I have to tell you this and you must believe me. If Mrs Brandi wasn't there, I would've jumped over the chairs and I would have attacked that girl and really done something terribly violent to her. As God as my witness. So help me. I would've seriously hurt that girl. But I kept my cool. I had to control myself. I walked out of that stage. Mrs Brandi immediately rushed to find me. I was on the lobby and sat one of the chairs. I sobbed and wept. Mrs Brandi found me. She kneeled and comforted me. She asked me what was wrong and I told her that I was having a headache. She could see that I was crying uncontrollably. She then suggested that I speak to a counselor. She went to a counselor's office. She told me to go speak with Mr Daniels. And I quietly went to his office. I spoke with him. Somehow, It was known all over the school by the end of that Friday. As I spoke to him through that time I was feeling better. I told him that I wanted to be an actor and I liked acting. Mr Daniels suggested a School in Winston-Salem, NC. The NC School of the Arts. Well, I was on the Bus going home to School, The kids were talking about what I did to that girl. Nobody bothered me.

But it wasn't over. I was still depressed and feeling low. I just wanted people to leave me alone. Yes, I knew it was wrong to do that to her. I was just lost. Just lost. Can someone help me??? And

Contacting my gang from "St Ann's School" didn't help much either. I was in a cage. I would call Maurice and Vincent. I was overly excited to see them and many others. I missed them terribly. Sadly enough, they would soon distance themselves from me.

Well, I got my report card, Jan-Feb, 1987. My grades was okay but it could've been much better. My Hyper mania was like me being an "alcoholic" in my mind. "Sour Sixteen", I would call this period in my life. Hell, I didn't even want to go to school. My Fear of getting "bullied" and having to defend myself was a constant struggle from time to time. One night, My sister Tonya and I was talking to me one night. She sensed that I was going through struggles at school and that I was in complete "loneliness" and a "Mess". But there was one thing she told me, "When you graduate from that school, you're not going to see those kids no more."

Still, My true passion was still the drums. I knew that I could've been a member of the Terry Sanford Band. At football and basketball games, I would see the band play. The Classic tune, "Tequila" with the Pee Wee Herman Dance. Seeing the Drummers march on the Football Field and in the Gym. I was thinking to myself, "I can do that". "I'm better than those drummers". The band was alright but not really good.

So, Feb-March, I had to take The NC Competency Test. Yes, Just like that Functional Skills Test I failed so miserably. I haven't gotten over that. Now, this examination, much like the he exam I took at Hillcrest, focuses on your Basic Math Skills, Reading and Writing Objective Skills. You have to pass in order to graduate. I took it. The results? I failed Both parts. Just missed a few points over the average score you must make. I didn't care about school anymore but I didn't want to let my parents down by not graduating.

Spring 1987 came along. The students had to register for classes next school year, 1987-1988. I wanted to register for Acting II, But Mrs Brandi approached to me. She didn't want me for Acting II. She didn't want to deal with me anymore because I was, "Bothering the girls too much." Evidently, it had to do what I did to the girl, hurling a book at her in a manic rage. It let me down even more and my self-esteem was very very low. I was feeling, "I couldn't do anything." My hopes not returning to Acting class just knocked me down. And that made me really depressed. I passed to the 11th grade and as I got my report card in the mail.

Summer was just like any other summer. Teasie was now living in Jacksonville, FLA, Her husband John was stationed there. My mother let Tonya and I to go with them for a month in a half. It was fun. I couldn't complain though. They stayed in an Apartment, My nephew Dante' was only 3 and he was going through those "Terrible twos and threes". He always wanted to compete with me with everything I do. I was growing up and looking "Husky built" for a kid of seventeen. I ate like a 'HOG'. As I mentioned earlier, I adored food. No Summer School for me this time. I can get to enjoy and relax that summer of '87.

Late August, Tonya and I came home. She had to get ready to return to NCSU. I had to get ready for the School I hated so much. Being honest, I wasn't ready for the 11th Grade. I was registering classes knowing that I couldn't handle. No motivation at all. I wanted to make a Big "YELL" for Help.

First day of school. I was depressed. I was depressed. I was depressed. I didn't care about nothing. It was like I was just there. I went to the board chart to look for my homeroom teacher. Mr Sampson. He was a short, burly looking man light-skin complexion man with a tiny mustache. Very Sarcastic and some of the White students called him, "George Jefferson" from the TV hit show, THE JEFFERSONS. But he was very fond of me. I think he noticed my behavior and he would always talk to me about the importance of getting an education.

Let me Explain about myself during this time. I was on the verge of "SNAPPING". I had so much Rage and feeling so down and depressed. I needed help. Some of my classmates knew it. This period, I grieved, wept in such agony as a troubled teen I just felt no one could understand me. I can take so much abuse from a person whatever the case maybe. My parents was trying to figure me out. I wanted to take it out on them. My love for the Drums was still there inside me. Fighting and Arguing with my parents. I was very irritable. Very irritable. Every day, I had an Extreme Built up Rage inside me. I couldn't fight back some of the low life Bullies because I would "Punk" out. I had homework that I didn't even do. Aside from that, I had my love of music. Listening to Heavy Metal all sorts of music. I Really liked LED ZEPPELIN. I skipped School constantly with some of the kids and got in trouble that I was sent to "In School Suspension" for a week. Twice! I smoked Marijuana with a few Kids just to make me feel Better Before going to class. The Manic Behavior I had was annoying my classmates to the point that I was a "Villain". I sure was.

My "St Ann's Crew" were going on with their lives. Enjoying high school. Football Games, Basketball Games. School Dances. The Bond with them was still there. Maurice Thomas and his Brother Willie would invite "the St Ann's crew" to their house and spend the weekend. Because their Birthdays were in September. Now my father had no problem with that. He didn't like some of those Boys I was trying to hang around with. From September 1986, 1987 and 1988, I went to all of them. THE FOUR HORSEMEN OF THE APOCALYPSE were there. Maurice invited Vincent Robinson and Derek Sellers but they never came. As for Vincent? He didn't want to be bothered by us. I know that Derek had his own struggles too but he was still my "Chum" from St Ann School. I always accepted those Kids. My loyalty was still there. Maurice's mother, so kind she didn't mind my father dropping me off to their house so early. We would eat Caesar's Pizza. Watch movies late at night. Playing Video Games on the Television. The next Morning on Sundays, Mrs Thomas would cook Breakfast for us. That was good. But there was tension within us. It was mostly the FOUR HORSEMEN OF THE APOCALYPSE. They all attended different schools and enjoying life as teens. They were growing up and had their own lives to live. But looking back, I strongly felt the "Loyalty and Bond" was slowly drifting away. Unfortunately, it will reach to the point they will shut the door in my face. Soon very soon. But the Bottom line was: I was lost.

As the new school year came by, I purchased a silver class ring. It was a very nice ring eventually, I lost it.

People, Things weren't going out just right in my life at that time. I was thinking and reminding to myself, "At that Christmas Musical that December night, I am the GIFT." I am someone. I am somebody.

Carla and I weren't speaking to each other. I guess she gave up on me. Because I was all out. Didn't realize that I needed help.

January 1988- Fayetteville had a big Wintry Blizzard that forced us out of school for 2 weeks. So, most of the time I was at home watching TV. Of course, I didn't do any homework. It took a long time for the snow to thaw out. Later that month, Schools all of Cumberland County resumed.

Feb-Mar 1988. I had to retake the NC Competency Test. For the second time, I failed. That was making me angry. I had to graduate by passing that Exam. Another Worry. Failing grades. A troubled youth. I felt like I was boiling. I just wanted to blow up. Explode.

Spring 1988. I was really having it out with my parents. I felt they couldn't understand me. Constant arguing, I was thinking about running away. It was one day, A Saturday, in May that I've almost reached the end of my rope with them. I talked with Eddie White on the phone. Now, I don't know if he heard me arguing with my parents but I told him that I was coming to his house. I hung up the phone. Quickly, I put on my shoes and walked out of the house. My Dad was asking me where are you going. I kept on walking fast but I was going to run. Run away. Run away, Travis. Well, I didn't get too far from my neighborhood. Dad caught me just in time, driving his car as I saw him. I got very very Angry!! "Get in the car," Dad said in command. I had no choice I got in the car. At home in our den, the arguing continued. Mom, Dad and Tonya (Spring semester was over for her. She will return in June). They all came at me. Mom starting hitting me and I blocked her hand. I wanted to hit her back. I was Yelling and I got up and furiously walked to my room. Then Dad was at me again, "What's wrong?", My Father pleading to me as he asked me that I burst into tears. I cried. I cried. I couldn't even express myself. But he told me to apologize to my mother. I did. To get my mind off things I did my homework. Or whatever I had to do. BUT! My troubles was not over. Not by a long shot. Those long desert sands....Raging Storms....And Robber Bands.....

Anyway, School was about to end in June. I was waiting to the last minute getting my school work done. Trying to make some good grades. I failed most of the classes. I had to go to Summer School again at Douglas Byrd Sr High. In my fragile state, I took Basic Math with a little Algebra. There were some Kids from my school that were in the class. A few from Westover High and 71st High. None of us got along. The kids knew that I had issues. A Troublesome Teen. But there was Hope! Vincent Robinson was there. He was very muscularly built. Still had that high pitched voice and With his short stature. He wasn't wearing his glasses anymore at that time. He was socializing with two guys. He knew alot of the kids there. During Lunch Break, I would go to him. But, in truth, He didn't want to deal with me.

Summer School was weary for me, I was so worried If I was going to pass or not. But my worries was over. I passed the class. Barely.

That Summer was a very troublesome for me because of my manic behavior. Late June I almost got arrested for trying to steal a Soldier's Hat at Ms Lugo's wedding. I attended her wedding which my family didn't approve of. Especially my Father. Actually, I wasn't even invited. Angela told me. Angela Butler, Matt Bradley, one of THE HORSEMEN OF THE APOCALYPSE were there. Her reception was held at this Officer's Club on Ft Bragg. After that incident, A military policeman and an officer came to my home. Yes, they did. My mother was getting anxious and mad. My Father and Tonya was watching TV in our den. They questioned me that I stoled the hat. I was nervous as hell. I told them that I didn't. My mother interrupted their questions when they asked. I found the Air Force hat and gave it to a Bartender. She was very nice about it. I called the bartender and asked her was the hat still there and she said yes. The Military Police Officer wasn't going to press charges on me. They wanted the Hat returned. My mother did the same thing and she said to that officer that I didn't steal it. It wasn't over. Tonya and Dad was asking me about what was going. Now, my father wasn't in our living room when they questioned me. If my father was in our living room, It would have been a different story.

What I did next was going to haunt me. I wrote this "Love Letter" to Ms Lugo's sister Patricia. I used Bible verses the Song of Psalms. Well, it rather frightened her and her Family. So, that late night, in August, Ms Lugo's mother called my house up and accused me of breathing on the phone that night which I didn't do. She was just going off on my father. My father went off on me. "What you doing sending letters to Ms Lugo and Calling and Breathin on the phone??" I replied that I didn't do that. He argued with me about that. So, I called Mrs Lugo and I admitted that I did write the letter. But I never called and breathing on the phone. With her thick accent, "You've gone too far this time, Travis". She threatened she will call the police on me if it continues. After that, My Father put it on the line. "LEAVE THEM ALONE!" "You always getting in trouble with that woman!" "Leave her Family Alone." That was it. I left them alone. It's over. YET!!! It wasn't over.

That week of August, things were still getting worse for me. That Friday, my father wanted me to cut grass. We were going to go visit my Grandmother. I was irritable of course, Tonya and I got into an argument. So, I went to the Back yard to our barn to get a pail of gasoline. Tonya was cooking French Toast. A kid I knew from my neighborhood, "Sam", I borrowed his bike as I walked to his house. I got his bike. And so I got his bike and rode to the Gas station. It was Hot that day. I always cautioned myself crossing the street. As I carefully, crossed Ramsey street and there was the gas station. I filled the plastic pail a $1.00. Still, irritable, I got on the bike. Carefully, I crossed the street. There was a bank, I rode to the Drive Thru, I was riding pretty fast but not too fast. Then I rode out of the Drive Thru. Then unexpectedly, a white or yellow Cadillac came and struck me as I as going to cross the street. I was hit hard. The Bike was really wrecked and damaged. I was in extreme pain from My lower back. Then the Man who drove his Cadillac came out of his car. "Are you okay, son?" I couldn't answer. I was in extreme Pain. Believe Me. All he did was grab my hand and pulled or I can say dragged me to the sidewalk on the grass. He got into his car and drove off. I never saw the man. So, a few witnesses came to me. There was a lady weeping. A man who was a yard worker witness the whole incident. An ambulance was called. The Police came by. I was nervous as hell. I spoke as the police officer questioned me. I was scared to death. Because, earlier that week, Ms Lugo's mother threatened to turn me to the police for a stupid letter I sent to her eldest daughter Patricia. Which was wrong. So the ambulance came. I was put on a stretcher and taken to Cape Fear Valley Hospital. I was unconscious a little bit but the pain in my back excruciating. My mother was there before my father. She was still calm and relaxed and my father was worried as hell. I got my lower back to X-Ray. When I was lying on the bed, the nurse had to lift me up and I just couldn't get up for him to take X-Ray pictures. He was very patient and somehow I got lower back X-Rayed in the room. So, I seriously sprained my lower back from the impact of the wreck. But my doctor wanted a sample of my urine to see if there was any blood. But there wasn't. So, I was taken home. And I had to have bed rest for 2 weeks. And School was about to start.

Well, my Dad had to settle out things of what happened. Yes, I was at Fault. Jay Walking. The Man who struck me wanted to sue me for wrecking his car. Though, he was never there for me when the ambulance came. He left. My Dad was in his room arguing on the telephone about what I told him. "I'll believe my son before I believe anybody." I was so nervous and worried about what my Father might do to me. And my Dad said, "That was something that just happened!" I was certain my Father was going to grab me. He didn't. That gave me a relief.

September 1988. My last School year at Terry Sanford Sr High. I was a SENIOR. Finally. But it went by so quickly. Very Fast. Still, I was in pain from my lower back. I didn't fully recuperate because My doctor strictly told me to rest in Bed for 2 weeks. But my mother insisted that I should go to school anyway. But the classes that I registered for was a CHANGE for me. I wanted to take Acting But

I couldn't. I had to take courses for remedial Reading/Writing and Math because of my failure from the NC/Competency Test. I hated that. I had no choice and it was mandatory. So, I had to put my feelings to the side and get on the Ball with this. I promised myself to pass that Examination with a High Score.

Okay, Being a Senior didn't really matter that much to me. All my Classmates were excited. And when they had plans on going to college. I didn't even know what to do. But that year, I really focused on my school work. Yes, Indeed. I didn't play around. But the issue about me what will I be doing when I leave high school??

I went to a counselor Mr Lawson and he told me that my grades were not strong enough for me to attend college. He was a kind man yet brutally honest.

Carla Douglas never spoke to me. Even when we on the bus we hardly spoke. I couldn't blame her. My Manic behavior was already noticeable at school. I let those Kids Get to me. They really got under my Skin. Now, I did have a few kids who were friendly to me. I couldn't lie about that. The bottom line was that I wanted to get the Hell out of that school. At home, I could do basically anything I want. I could stay up a little to 10:30-11:00pm. But I had to be in Bed after finishing my homework. Friday Nights, I watched LATE NIGHT WITH DAVID LETTERMAN on NBC. I had to watch that. It was the Talk of the School. I loved Watching David Letterman with his clumsy, obnoxious self. I taped some of his Episodes on our VCR. I enjoyed watching him being sarcastic and annoying people in Downtown New York.

December 12, 1988. I was an Uncle again. My niece Demi was born. I was happy and proud for my sister Teasie. She always wanted a girl. Christmas arrived, Teasie and her Family came to visit us and we saw the little babe niece of mine. It was joyous. Even, my Grandmother, "Grand Ma Daisy" came to have Christmas dinner with us. I got a camera because I was taking pictures of the Family.

1989 has finally arrived. I was thinking about going to that NC School of the Arts and that Acting School in NY. Really, Travis? Really??? You know your parents were not letting you go to NY. I had Family there. But that was a "NO, NO". Period. I wanted to join the Military. There were Armed Forces recruits coming to our school wanting young men and women to join Uncle Sam. I already registered with the Selective Service when I turned eighteen last June. I wanted to be a LEATHER NECK. A JARHEAD. A MARINE. Dad wasn't having it. I have to worry and focus on passing that NC Competency Test so I can graduate.

After the Months of having being prepared in those classes and taking sample tests to get ready for Exam. I was ready.

Feb-Mar. I got off the Bus at school and went straight to the cafeteria to take the NC/Competency Test. I let nothing stand in my way. My mind was centered on passing this Exam. When the instructors were present and The Exam was given to the kids. I got to it.

I PASSED IT! I busted with a Score 100 on the Writing Objective and 97 on the Math!!

April 1989 arrived and it was time for the Prom or whatever you want to call it. Long Story short, I met this kid who was a "Complete Phony". Looking Back, I think he was a Hustler. He wanted to join the Marines. "Randy" who had really bad Breath. We both decided to go to the prom. We rented Tuxedos. He had a Black One and I had a White one with a pink tie. I looked so Damn awkward. He had a girl to go with him. I asked a few girls but I got turned down. We rented a car so we can take turns driving. The Prom came. It was held at the Holiday Inn. I danced hardly with any girl. After the Prom, we went to the International House of Pancakes on Bragg Blvd, with a few classmates. We ordered dinner and "Randy" had no money at all. I had to pay for everything. The friendship was over. He tried to apologize of what happened. I didn't accept it all. I think about week after the Prom, he Vanished. A few Boys approached to me and asked me have I seen him or not. I said No. He stoled money not only from me but a few other boys. I guess he was a marked guy. I don't care. The Hell with him.

May 1989. Graduation was fast approaching. There was an incident that involved the death of a student. He got accepted to

Fayetteville State University. He was called "BIRD". I really don't know the details about his death because it was baffled and confusing. It really put stain on our school. I had one class with him, Earth Science when I was a Junior. I knew who he was but not personally. My condolences goes to his family and may he rest in Peace.

June 6, 1989, I graduated From Terry Sanford Sr High. It was held at the Cumberland County Auditorium. There was a party later that night at the Holiday Inn on Owen Drive. I didn't go. I was through with that school. I was upset that Tonya couldn't make it to my graduation. She came home late with Sivi Collins. My parents went to my graduation. I Got my diploma. It was done and Dealt with. It was over.

I graduated from High School. Now What??

Again, I was feeling empty. The scars from Terry Sanford high school never left me. It was also making me very angry. There was nothing that school offered me. Except misery.

So, my parents sent me to go to Maryland to visit my sister Teasie. John was stationed at Patuxent River Naval Air station. A Base with Navy Sailors and Grunt Marines. I stayed there the whole summer. Actually, since I was a visitor, I was supposed to be there for a week not for 4 months, (July-Nov).

Yes, Teasie and John saw my symptoms. Teasie and Tonya were worried if I had the same mental disorder as Mom. During that time I was there I had to get a job and I did. I worked at the BQ, Cleaning the headquarters and doing the laundry. I had to work there everyday. To be honest, I wasn't quite ready to do any work. But I was mostly lazy and not doing my work. So, I applied at another job, McDonald's. Really, I worked there but a manager wanted me fired. I met some real good people there at that base. But the thing was they saw something odd in me. They would see me "talking and rambling to myself" that I was troubled young teen. That was the truth. "He talks to himself."

As my brief time working at the BQ, I quit. So, I stayed at McD's. On the Base, Dante' and his sister Demi went to pre-school and Teasie worked in Washington DC. She had to get up early in the morning to catch the Bus and ride there to her job. John worked on the base of course. John and Teasie dealt with my issues and they knew it.

So, I returned home that Nov. John and Teasie left for Bermuda. Shortly after returning home, Fayetteville was renovating The Prince Charles Hotel.

I was looking for employment. I applied to the so-called "Prince Charles Hotel". The hotel was still in construction in Dec, 1989 in downtown Fayetteville. I applied for position "Bus Boy". Got Hired. I was suprised. I was wandering around not doing my job. My bosses were harassing me. And a punk I went to Terry Sanford was working with me. While they were working and building the Hotel, it was not finished. Incomplete. Foolishly, they opened the hotel on New Year's Eve. Me? Working as Bus Boy, I tried but I had my times. One my boss' assistant told me, "William, you're like Night and Day." I worked at Chloe's Restaurant. The Head chefs were not all that nice. Especially, the Head chef. He was a Big Fat whale with a thick accent. The food was not all that good, except their Breakfast Brunch which held on Sundays. The waitresses did their work. But the bosses were "too flirty" with the girls. Yes, I did the same thing too. I wasn't innocent. I got into some serious trouble with one girl whose mother told me to leave her alone. Actually, I didn't do anything to her. But I left her alone.

There was one lady that worked as a receptionist and cashier. A quiet Afro-American woman in her late forties. She noticed my behavior. No lie. I was very cruel and moody towards her. She tried to talk to me. I would walk away from her. I would roar at her. Take make a long story short, it was one Saturday morning, I was in my irritable moods. She wanted me to take up the breakfast to a customer in their room. I scoffed at her very bad and took the order to the room. That was it. My Boss wanted to talk to me. Told me flat out and gently, "You're going home." I thought I was fired. I didn't work for a few days and I came back to look at my schedule and I returned to work. I had to calm myself. So, I worked at Chloe's for 2 ☐ months and I quit in March 1990.

I went to Edwards Music on McPherson Church Road. I resumed my studies playing the drums. I got my red snare drum from three piece drum set. Mr Bob Williams knew I was advanced at the drums. However, he suggested that I learn the classical guitar. That was more challenging. I thought that was impossible. But He would tell me, "I know you could do it."

I remember Mr Lawson, the counselor at Terry Sanford. He told me that I should attend Fayetteville Tech Community College. But I wanted to return to my love for the drums and I did. I went back to Edwards Music and I knew of Bob Williams, Guitar instructor and had a wide range of Knowledge of Music. Since, I just only Had a Snare drum, He taught me the basic rudiments of the drums. I felt better but I wanted a Whole drum set. But Mr Williams insisted that I should play the Classical Guitar.

So, I took a chance but it would be a long journey. I was purchasing the wrong guitar. It was an acoustic. I tried. I practiced and I was getting frustrated. But as the time passed by when I would have lessons with him. It was his wide knowledge of music that impressed me. His wife played the piano. A very nice lady, I had the utmost respect for her and his two sons who was musically talented as well. All that I can say was that he was so patient of me.

I studied Art back in '88. The Arts Instructions School in Minneapolis, MN. I applied there and my parents paid for it. I love Art so much as I mentioned to you earlier at first I wanted to be a Biblical Artist like Richard and Frances Hook. I got so frustrated that I had no patience for it. I quit. I did disappointed my parents and I'm very sorry that I didn't complete my studies.

Days went by and I had no motivation. During the time, I was going through depression. I wanted to do so much. After, I graduated from High school, I was still depressed that I couldn't attend College. I couldn't get over high school. I just couldn't. I had issues and problems. Believe me on that. As everyone, I knew everybody else was going on with their lives. I didn't and couldn't.

So, Sept 1990. I got a job as a Bus Boy at Chi-Chi's on McPherson Church Road. I started working there. I wasn't there long because I wasn't productive. I wandered and walking around the restaurant. And I was flirting with the Girls (which I shouldn't been doing). There was one manager that didn't like me Because I was trying to get up with this girl who attended Methodist University. That really pissed him off. So, He summoned me on flirting with girls. I worked there only Three weeks. He called me to his office for the last time and he said, "I'm sorry". I knew that I was fired.

It bothered me alot. Some of my employees were upset supporting me saying I was doing my job. But that Boss didn't see it that way.

Now, this period in my life where I was going through serious stigma. It was going to be a very traumatic period in my life. I was slowly declining. I didn't realize that I needed help.

Late Nov. 1990, I got hired by McDonald's on Bragg Blvd. My family was Happy for me. But they were going to relocate further up Bragg Blvd. It was a new MC DONALD'S. I was ready to work there. I worked there in Maryland and that gave me experience. During those years (1990-1995) being employed there it was a rollercoaster for me.

Dec 1990-Feb-1996 was the last period in my life that the symptoms of my highly manic behavior took it's toll on me. I will go through extreme Stigma. Persecution, Prejudice and Ignorance. I was in a boat that was sinking. I would have endure the name that I highly, strongly abhor and detest, CRAZY.

My friends from St Ann's would eventually shut me out. Not realizing that they didn't want to deal with me anymore. They shut the door in my Face. Sadly, disowning me. I would get "Bit" by the most of my co workers at McDonald's. Rejection. Thrown away. Being taken advantage of.

As, I worked at McDonalds on the grill. Flipping Hamburgers. Making Biscuits, Big Macs and Egg Mc Muffins. It was an occasional thing. First, I liked it. But with my Behavior it led me to have frictions and difficulty working with them. Some were fearful of me because of my "extreme moodiness". Towards the end I hated it. During this period, I was not getting any sleep. Yet, there were some good people. I would let my managers argue with me Because I didn't have the courage to defend myself. Verbal abuse. They threatened to terminate me. Yes, I did a lot of flirting with the girls but they did the same to me. They would have their moods and throw that "sexual harassment" issue on me. Yes, I had to back off. Because they would Win and I would lose.

Though I did my work. Working on the Grill gave me a lot of experience. I always have to work on the morning shift. I was very very moody. I was so moody that you couldn't get a "GOOD MORNING" out of me. My Bad attitude. So as I was working, I wanted to go to California. I always did. So, Sept. 1990, I called up **PIONEER ELECTRONICS** in Long Beach, CA. I struck up a conversation with a girl and asked her things about California. She says it's wonderful living there. I started it. She told me her name was "Sheera". She was so surprise to learn that I was from N. Carolina. So she told me a bit about herself. She's from Sri Lanka (Ceylon) and lived in California since she was a kid. Her parents worked at Northrop. A company that manufactures parts for aeroplanes and other accessories. We exchanged our addresses. And in extreme impulsivity, I got to writing countless letters to her. Telling her about myself. Well, we just talked on the phone. She first sent a letter and a picture to me. She was Beautiful. She was 26. I continued to writing letters to her. Later that Fall, She calls me and she was somewhat rude and profane. She said she wanted a "Friendship". Now that didn't go well with me. That was not what I wanted. I wanted more. She had a ex-boyfriend she seriously dated for 6 years. She was still emotionally attached to him and he was still calling. She went through her period of "finding herself". She had an older Brother, whom I must say had a taste for being a real good dresser. Now this was the 90's okay? She had an younger sister who was very beautiful. She was a year older than me.

I shared with my problems what I going through but she assured me that she would "lean on me". Still, she kept on emphasizing that this is nothing but a "Friendship". So, the next Year 1991, We both arranged for me to travel to California. I went to "Maupin Ttravel" and I met my travel agent, her name was Jeanine Bergman. She was from Patterson, New Jersey and her husband was in the Military. A mother of 2 children. She was an legit travel agent. Anything I asked her, She knew it right off the Bat. As a matter of fact, I tested her from Conde Nast Travel Magazine. There was an article on 10 questions you should ask your travel agent. She answered everyone of them. We both got along well partly because her Birthday was in June. Like mine. She was a short, petite young dark Brunette forty-something woman with a lovely face and a fantastic smile. I really liked her a lot. She was a great inspiration on me like Lori Hoskins.

As I was getting ready for our trip, Tonya was getting concerned about me talking to someone on the phone in our new guest room. I told her about this "Girl from California" I met over the phone.

Spring 1991. Since, I was contacting her. "Sheera" did sensed that I was "overly sensitive", she was becoming more comfortable with me. She sent me more photos of herself and Family which was good. As we continued to talk over the phone, she was always bringing up her ex-boyfriend from time to time. And that highly Angered me. And this was the start of us having serious differences and arguments.

She had this selfish, spiteful attitude; "I don't do nothing to no one. I don't live on egg shells. I don't apologize. I just go on with my life. I'm not responsible for your wants and needs."

I should've sensed that But I had to learn the Hard way. Believe me. That morning, before my mother took me to the Fayetteville Municipal Airport, My Father came to me in my room and he put his arms on my shoulders, "Don't go out there Falling in Love."

May 8, 1991-May 22, 1991. I traveled to California to see my "Dream Girl" or whatever you want to call it. I left Fayetteville to Raleigh then Georgia to Texas and then to Texas California. I arrived at the LAX Airport. It wasn't long before I saw Sheera. I was so happy to see walk through the terminal and we embraced. Maybe I was too happy. Now, since I saved my money, Sheera suggested that I stay at her house. Her parents had a death in their Family and they had to traveled to their native Sri Lanka. I got to her house. It was really nice. The China Wear and the Den. I met her sister, "Kara" and her cousin "Maria". I met her Brother. I was overly and highly

highly manic to see her that it annoyed her. I wanted to do nothing but to impress her.

So, those two weeks that I visited her, I really began to see her "True self". Always talking about her ex-boyfriend. Yes, he didn't live that far from her. I had some good times with her. But symptoms were being noticeable. But I was with my "Dream Girl". We went to amusement parks, Knots Berry Farm and Magic Mountain. As I was there, she showed me her Family Photos when they first came to California as well pictures of her Family at her native Sri Lanka.

She, her sister and Kara were very hospitable to me. Sheera could sense that I was very troubled. The only time that she had the most compassion when she took me out to this Beach and we talked. She made it plain that I needed someone to talk to. But she kept bringing her ex-boyfriend up from time to time. Her sister, "Kara" and I got along very well. She was just 22 and I was still 20. We talked about movies and music. She knew her way in the Los Angeles area. Though Sheera lived in Gardena which was outside LA. There were times she was getting frustrated around the house. She threw a party at her house But I was feeling really out of place and insecure. I was quiet and rambling to myself. The Bottom line was I just wanted to be with her. Towards the last days I stayed with her I was definitely making her uncomfortable. Yes, it was one night, she was making snide remarks about her wanted to be with her ex-boyfriend. Later that night, I tried to make a move at her and she told me plainly, "I don't respond to your feelings." It was a rejection. Point Blank. Since I was so blind and fragile, I just wanted to let her know that I really cared for her. I guess it didn't matter to her. And she was becoming difficult and cruel towards me. The Last night that I was at her house, I could not sleep. So, I had to return home. As she drove me back to the Airport, I was getting emotional and weeping. But she cheered me up, "Well, there's always the phone", Sheera said. We took our last picture together. I left to go to my terminal, I saw her one last time and she waved at me. I never saw her again.

I came home to N.Carolina. Tonya and Dad were at the airport to pick me up. I was told that McDonalds wanted me to return to work as soon as possible and I did. But Sheera was always on my mind. At McDonald's, I was really feeling miserable. I had serious arguments with my Supervisor "Sally". She always on my case that summer of '91. Sally threatened she was going to fire me. I asked her about a raise and she replied and looked at me, "I know you ain't asking me about no raise." As she rolled her eyes and walked away. But I was thinking about "Sheera".

Sheera's Birthday was in late June. I just turned 21 and She turned 27. So, I went out my way to buy her flowers for her Birthday. So, as the time passed, I kept contacting her. We were arguing on the phone and not getting along. Later that year, Sept. She called me up and told me that she has a "New" Boyfriend. I felt a painful churn in my stomach. I was hurt. We Argued and Argued. I was terribly hurt.

So, one day in September, I woked up. I looked up in ceiling. It was spinning around. My Head was Spinning like a Merry-go-round. I got up and my room was spinning. And I had to work that afternoon. It was very agonizing.

So, Still, I was sending Sheera senseless "Love Letters". Most of the times we called each other, we constantly argue. Towards the end of the Year. It was getting senseless. It reached the point she was teasing me. Knowing how "overly sensitive' She kept rubbing it on. Until Tonya had a long talk with me just saying stop contacting her. I didn't do immediately. And I was still suffering Vertigo. I continued to send letters but there was nothing that I could do.

Things wasn't improving with my co-workers and I. Especially with Sally. That November, I had to report to work at 6am-2pm. It was on a Saturday. I was the only employee working on the Grill area. Sally was helping me out. We argued more than we worked together. The Breakfast Rush was kicking. Busy. Very Busy. I was everywhere. Keeping the food in the stand area. We almost ran out of Biscuits. My lower back was aching me. The transfer Breakfast to Lunch was always hectic. Sally was verbally abusive to me. I knew that I argue back she will fire me on the spot. I didn't get a break. It was just that busy. During the early afternoon Rush was Hectic. Customers were crowded in the Lobby. I was getting very tired and exhausted. Finally, 2 o'clock approached, nobody still showed up for work. I worked overtime. And I was getting irritable. But I kept my cool for so long. So, as things slowed down for Lunch. The Afternoon crew came all laughing and carrying on. Taking their sweet time clocking on. It was 3 pm. I worked my shift and I wanted to clock out and go home. Sally, being really harsh told me to empty the trash from the grill area. Unfortunately, I didn't get to clock out yet. She was avoiding me. With her "Sista Attitude". Walking away from me. I did everything she told me to do but still she refused to let me go. Now, this was an incident that could've ceased. Stopped. As the afternoon crew clocked on. I told Betsy that I was finished taking out those Bags of trash. Sally yelled, "You ain't going nowhere until you empty all this trash." Terry, who was newly promoted "Swing Manager", I'll never forget this and I must share it with you to understand my side of the story. After Sally roared and yelled at me that instant. A few employees laughed. Timothy looked at me. Terry looked at me. Threw his hands up and smiled at me as if to say, "She's the Boss. There's nothing I could do." THAT TRIGGERED IT!!! Impulsive and filled with rage I grabbed the metal grill scraper. Anything I could get my hands on. I was going to attack Sally, my Supervisor. Timothy and a few employees were shocked when they saw what I going to do. They knew I SNAPPED AND I WAS GOING TO HER ASS!! "I'm gonna Hurt Somebody!!, I yelled. Immediately, Terry and a few others tried to calm me down. "Hold on, Man!" "Chill, Chill!" Calm down Man!". Sally saw my rage and displeasure. They quickly took the Grill Scraper away from my hands and I went to the Break room. I was ANGRY!! I WAS ANGRY!! I WAS ANGRY!! So, as I was in the Break room. I really had to calm down. It was pushing 4 o'clock. Sally came inside and said to me gently, "We do appreciate your help." She walked out the Break room looking shocked. I clocked off and my father picked me up and I went home. Enough Said.

Yes, It was the talk at the store among the employees about the incident. Frictions continued between Sally and I as the employees looked on. But Later that December, she got demoted to Assistant Manager and relocated to the McDonald's at Hope Mills.

December 1991. Christmas was not very good for me. Sheera and I still argued over the phone. I was depressed. The only good thing that came out of it was my Nephew Dante', age 7 and my niece Demi, just turned 3 years old was growing up. I got sick with a sore throat and I had the flu.

January 1992. I wanted to have my own Car because my mother did not want me to drive our Gray Buick Regal and my mother was declining in her mental health.

As far as contacting Sheera, that was going to end. As I said before, it was getting nowhere. I shared my issues about that with a few people and They told it's not going to work. I slowly distant myself from her and writing letters about what's going on in my life. I tried one last time and like a Fool, I bought another set of Flowers for Easter that April. She had her own life and had someone in her life. So, that early May, She called me up and told me she liked the flowers. She took some pictures by her father but they came out bad. Then she mentioned her Boyfriend and abruptly I came to the conclusion just to leave her alone. I ended the conversation immediately. That was it. I decided to stop corresponding to her. The aftermath was that I picked up negative vibes and it was really a burden to me. I had to move on.

Jan.1993, Sheera calls me up all of a sudden. I knew that I was going to confront her one last time. It was almost a year since she heard from me. It was the same 'ol song. She started her sarcasm and told me she got married. It didn't hurt me one bit but I was shook up. I just went on defense to her. We started exchanging words. Yes, she asked me about my Family and all that. Again, I ended the conversation quickly and abruptly. Two Days later, She calls me again as my mother was in the kitchen. I just went into a rage and I told that I felt mistreated by her. She never respected me. It escalated to an argument again. Yes, All that she had on me that she let me stay at her house. I wanted to stay in a hotel. I had enough money. Just to let you know that. I never asked her if I could stay with her. I was manic and loud on the phone with her. I couldn't get my point across but she did listen and I felt shut out. I had No intentions whatsoever of contacting her back. It was over. Done and Dealt with. Later that Summer, Tonya talked to me about her and she told me that Sheera called her when I was a work and she showed her "True colors" when it came to me. Putting me down. Saying her Ex-Boyfriend was jealous of her letting me stay at her house. That they might get back together. Wondering why I was so "Sensitive". Tonya told me that she never liked her. She was relieved that I stopped contacting her. All that I picked up from that experience was Negative Vibes as I mentioned earlier. It took a long time for me to recover from that. I was only protecting myself those last two times she called me and it just made very very angry. Miserable. Later, I got all of the pictures we both took when I was a California. The letters. Postcards and a framed picture of her in my room she first sent me. I burned all of it in our back yard. It was my way of healing my hurt.

Now, as I was having my falling out with Sheera. Things was loosening up for me. A little bit. That April 1992. I purchased my first Car. A turquoise Blue 1992 GEO-METRO XFI. A stick. My friend Sonny from work taught me drive the stick But it was Craig Douglas who taught me how to drive on the Road. I was nervous but he assured everything was fine. I loved that Car. There's nothing like having your own Transportation. PERIOD.

That summer of 1992 wasn't good at all for me or my family. My mother had another Breakdown which made her lock herself in our bathroom. Dad was so worried, emotional and was weeping. We called the Police. Mom was still in the Bathroom and she said nothing. We thought she committed suicide or least harmed herself. A few of our neighbors came wanting to know what's going on. As the police called for her to unlock the bathroom. She was extreme profane. Cursing and Shouting. Telling the police to get out her house. And they did. Before they left, they wanted to know if she's alright. Eventually, she got out of the Bathroom. Our guest room was like a tornado hit. Clothes were scattered everywhere. Tonya was with my mother as she comforting her on the bed. We had no choice but to send her to a mental hospital. As we went to take her mom had her head down while riding in the Car. It took a long time to get her in. Mom was suddenly aware what was going on. As we left, as the nurses took her. She was screaming directly at Tonya, "What are you doing?" "Why you doing this to me?" "You ain't my daughter!!" It really didn't affect me at all. I was sad and I understood everything. Tonya was weeping and crying. Dad, Strong as he was kept himself together as he drove us back home.

My mother stayed at the Cape Fear Valley Mental Health Center for close to two weeks. Mom wanted to go home. Her Doctor Mendez prescribed her medicine and she diagnosed as Schizophrenic. She still was struggling issues from her past that I can't share with you in my book.

At the drama at McDonald's, Again, I was irritable and moody during the rush. Now this was from time to time. But I just hated working morning shift. Nobody wanted to. I worked from 5am-1pm, 6am-2pm. There were Times I couldn't get any rest. The New Supervisor, Janet was another headache. But she was very good on what she did. Well, she a lot to do and It was her job. She was tough, in my opinion, she worked me to death. She knew that I was excellent on the Grill. I guess she expected us to give our 100% as a crew team. What I highly disliked about her was that she didn't know how to talk to people. She snaps at you. Though, honestly she was fond of me. She sensed that I didn't like working there. Everybody did. They knew my rollercoaster Moods. It reached to the point everybody was against me. Making my co-workers uncomfortable. Dealing with the Stigma. When will this ever end for me?

Now, I didn't have a lot of experience dating girls. Most of the time, I would get rejected terribly. Led on. When I was my "High Moods", I would flirt with the girls on the job. But they would do the same to me. Then, I'll be on my Days that I would argue with them. I was making them uncomfortable and I didn't even realize it.

Fall 1992, I registered Classes at FTCC because I wanted to attend College But I had to take the necessary courses to Transfer. Pre-Algebra. Algebra I and College Math. English/Reading. It was tough I was all by myself. Going to Work Early and Taking Evening Classes was another burden for me. Two Years earlier, I took the SAT. My Score was horribly. That wasn't the NC Competency Test.

I met a few good people there. That had study groups at their homes. I enjoyed some of the instructors. As for my Family, Mom was home that Fall But she was still stubborn. Let me just give it to you Straight; Mom never like going to the hospital. Never liked going for appointments or check-ups. Bottom Line.

I was frustrated at work. My co-workers arguing with me. Keep putting food in the bend. "Allen" was a former classmate from Terry Sanford High School. We never had classes together but we knew of each other. Well, it started off kind of bad. I was so scarred and feeling extremely bitter at my experience at Terry Sanford Highschool. I had no intentions of seeing any of them again. He noticed that I was avoiding him when we both worked together. Then one day, I was having my Break and he tried to talk to me. Again I avoided and ignored him. Allen couldn't take it anymore so he grabbed me and I refused. It was a struggle as he pushed me to the wall. "What's your problem?" He furiously asked. I didn't answer him back. But I wanted to get hands off of me. I walked from him. It took time for us to get acquainted again. We talked about High School. "I didn't do anything to you", He told me straight up. Now, he was sensing that I was having issues about that school and a lot of things. As I got to know him and we talked around at the Grill Area. I was slowly drawn to him. Then eventually, we became friends. We both helped each other and we hung out together. Also, he helped me with my Math homework when I was a FTCC. Allen was smart. Mostly, he was a "laidback" guy.

Back home, Mom was doing better but she was still being difficult. We had to take her back to the Hospital again but this time it made no sense. At that hospital, there were nice people. They knew my mother wasn't a sociable person. I had to be understanding that those people were struggling with Mental Disorders. But the patients were some characters there. One Big Guy would come and sign in anytime he wanted. He struck me as being Funny. Being the Center of Attention. There was one lady when I was visiting mom, she told my mother, "Geraldine, you lucky. You got a have a Family take care of you!" My mother was blessed because if that would've been any other Family. They would left her there. Point Blank.

Christmas 1992 was much better than last year. My Family had a good time. We all did. Especially, my nephew and niece. By the next year, 1993, I was still struggling with learning the Classical Guitar. It was going to take some real time learning it. Mr Bob Williams would always tell me. "I knew you could do it."

But my hyper manic behavior was still being bringing me down. My co-workers knew my ways, indeed. I was still highly respected by some of the kids. But point majority of them did not like me. Towards the end, I was becoming the "Villain" "WILL BATES" after Norman Bates from the Hitchcock thriller Classic, "PSYCHO". I didn't like being called those names by my co-workers and the managers. "CRAZY ASS".

One day, I called Allen and he was very blunt with me. "Yes you do bother people." He was giving me advice. Friendly Advice for me to stop having a negative attitude. Stop having the managers going against me. Well, an incident came one day at Mother's day. I put in a request DAY OFF that Sunday. So, that morning, they called me up and told me I had to be at work. I argued and I went in a Blind Rage. Put on my uniform and walked out of the house. Got in my GEO-METRO XFI and drove off. As I arrived there, Veronica was there to unlock the door and she saw my Facial expression. She was thinking, "Uh-Oh", something's going to happen here." I yelled and argued. My managers, Susan and Eric was trying to calm me down but I wasn't having it. "William, you would be fired if Janet was here!" Eric shouted 'HEY!! HEY!!. I stopped and he told me to go to the Crew Room. A few minutes after that, Eric came and talked to me. I was wearing down and I broked down with emotions. I just got a lot of my chest. Eric talked to me and told me it was my attitude that prevented me from being promoted Crew Trainer. I apologized to Susan and Eric. Later that summer, I got a raise and became a Crew Trainer. That's what I wanted anyway.

Allen and I were becoming more the best of friends than ever. The co-Workers at McD's thought we were Brothers. But he sensed that I was deeply troubled but he always assured me, "Don't worry about it."

So, during the summer of 93 was real hot. Goodness. Prior to Summers of 91-92, the weather news issued a Heat Weather Advisory. Stay Home. Now, Tonya was struggling to find a job. She worked at the Cumberland County Headquarters Library, she didn't like working there. Gossiping Ladies. Always starting drama. She worked there for awhile until she applied for a teaching position. Eventually, she would become a teacher to this day.

By the end of that year, I was still being a student of Mr Williams trying my Damndest to play the classical Guitar. I enjoyed being a student of Mr Williams. Sometimes, we talked about Musicians and music, generally. We talked about anything but he knew that I was stressed out working at McD's. Bob Williams was a true person and friend who I could talk to. He meant a lot to me.

That November, I took a little vacation with my Family. We went to Atlanta, GA, to watch the Dallas Cowboys take on the Atlanta Falcons. It was relaxing and fun. When I had ample time I got to practising my Guitar. But I had no motivation. I was feeling like I wasn't accomplishing anything. I simply had no interest in doing anything.

Groggy and tired from work I felt like everything was going down on me. Saturday Evening, November 6, 1993, my Family was planning a Birthday party for my Mother. It was after a funeral, So My sister Teasie, who just returned from Bermuda. John and Teasie cooked a dinner. It was a Feast indeed. I had to go home and set up the Balloons. Getting everything ready. My Father called the house and he told me that my mother was ready to come home. I was so happy that my mother's sisters came. They helped me out. Teasie, John, and their children, Dante', 9 and Demi, 4. My mother's sisters: Juanita, Doretha and her daughter Diane, Lueretta and much to my surprise Mrs Collins (Sivi's mother, Tonya's childhood friend) was their. My father's Family came. Christine, 'Uncle D' or "D.W., Uncle

Mac, Aunt Delores (Lois) and Aunt Bronnie and her husband Uncle David. Uncle Dora, Uncle Mayfield, And my dad's cousin's Earl Brown and "Billy". My mother wasn't expected this. But it was all lovely. My only regret was that Dante' forgot to get his video camera. UGHHHHH!!! And of course, they talked about the good 'ol days growing up as kids. I was so surprised that all my father's siblings were there. Yes, my father was juiced up a little bit. His Brother "Uncle D" was the life of the party. Fussing and arguing as a Family but it was all good. Tonya and I were talking about later that night. And the days proceeding.

As December rolled by, I was still taking classes at FTCC. Christmas rolled by. We had Christmas dinner at Teasie's house. I was very tired and restless, I took a much needed nap that afternoon. Working at McD's, Grrrr!!!

1994, The New Year arrived. I was becoming sick with the flu using that Vaporizing cream. It only made me worse. I was really sick. Even at work, my co-workers could tell I was becoming sick. I had the chills and shivering. So, I stayed home the next day. I went to the clinic. Doctor's Urgent Care on Owen Drive. I told my doctor that I had the sore throat. So, she subscribed to me some Strong Motrin. Back Home, I was in my Bed. People, I was feeling miserable. Coughing terribly. Tossing and turning. The medicine didn't actually didn't work about a day or two. That was the 24 hour Flu virus, I was fighting. I was never really sick like that since I was at St Ann School. Slowly, the medicine was working and I was getting better. Even, my managers at McD's called to check up on me. Well, they were concerned.

I was getting better and I washed my bed sheets and clothes. I had to return to work. Yeah, I had to return to work. Getting back into the swing of things. My Moody Behavior was still being tolerated. Well, I was trying not to be nuisance. One morning, "You're Moody, William," said Janet. Besides, Hanging out with my Friend Allen. I still had Maurice Thomas. He was at Fayetteville State University. He enjoyed his time there. He reached out to me as his Family always did. Since, I was a student at FTCC, I had a few privileges. I went to the Dances and somewhat having a good time. Trying my best to socialize with people. Maurice already knew my behavior. But he was there for me.

Bob Williams, My guitar instructor was telling me about that school because I was applying to a school in Winston-Salem. He was teaching me a little Music theory. He was telling to me not to go there. It's a different atmosphere. He gave me an example. If you're in a band or with your music instructor and you're playing your instrument, You better sight read those notes. And you ask your instructor, "What's that black note with a stem and flag thing with it?" You're going to get booted out." Mr Williams explained to me. I was stubborn. He was warning that I wasn't ready for college. It didn't matter if you listened to Classical, Jazz or modern contemporary music we listen today. The student must be musically literate.

I was trying to have a social life. Going out to clubs. A few of them. Most of the times, I would get a few dances from Girls but I get turned down. I was pitiful. Night life in Fayetteville, NC sucked. Only if you're a soldier from Ft Bragg, you got it made with the girls. Macho Bullshit. The soldiers were really ignorant at clubs. Fights were taking place. Girls getting knocked up by their boyfriends or guys they know. The girls trying to be something that they're not. "I GOTTA MAN!" Who the fuck cares? I don't. I was really feeling out of place. Nobody wasn't noticing anything about me besides my manic behavior but I was really sad and hurt. But I was different. A Menace to society. A disgrace. A loser. Crazy. Was there any hope for me???

The Gift, Part II

Mr Williams still insisted that I should play Classical Guitar. He cracked jokes and playing his classical Guitar. But there was once piece he was playing that really moved me. It sounded like two guitars playing at the same time. I asked him about that piece he was playing. He responded, "Recuerdos de Alhambra". A lovely classical piece of music. During that spring, we exchanged favors. He knew my taste in music. I ask him about certain musicians and styles of music. I would give him tapes or I'd record our lessons. But it was all about him anyway. I didn't mind. He knew that I was stressed out working at McD's.

Yes, I was the villain there. Allen was always there for me. I was really depressed. Depressed. Being rejected by a few a girls who were uncomfortable around me. I just felt. Empty. So, I approached my Supervisor Janet that I needed to take time off. Of all the work early in the Morning. Pulling 7-8 hours. Terribly restless and having no interest in doing anything. So, she gave me like a week off. I went to the Cumberland Co. Mental Health near downtown Fayetteville. I shared my problems with a counselor. She only told me, "You're just stress out from work. That all." And I went to the Cumberland Hospital near the Cape Fear Medical Center, A nice young lady I spoke to me and she said the same thing. But deep inside. I knew that I was suffering from some kind of mental issue. I was in denial.

Summer of 1994, was another tough time for me. Constantly arguing with my co-workers. My friendship with Allen was being tested too. In Jeopardy. He got promoted to Swing manager. I was studying him. But that was his new Job. We were always at your necks. I would give him looks. Some of the people saw it. Yes, Allen had power. He gave orders and sometimes I would mock him. One time, He summoned me to the office and talked but it was more like we were getting into fights. But we didn't. One morning, it was very busy. A customer ordered 24 Bacon, Egg and Cheese Biscuits. I prepared them but to Allen it wasn't fast enough. It almost escalated to a physical confrontation. Again, we argued. He was bold enough to call me. Accusing that it was my fault that he holding on to them. We exchanged words over the phone later that evening. I couldn't believe him. This was my friend and he's turning on me. I know he had a lot of responsibilities. We weren't respecting each other. Yes, He was doing his Job but he didn't have to take it out on me.

It reached to the point I wasn't getting along with anybody because of my constant mood swings. I never smiled and you couldn't get a "Good Morning" out of me. Irritable. As the summer past, and autumn arrived, October, I was making Biscuits. It was the last straw. Janet called me into the crew room and she had a real serious talk with me. I was drawn out, tired and highly exhausted. Janet told me that she couldn't handle me anymore and that all she could do was transfer me to another McD's restaurant. I felt I wasn't appreciated. I had to sign a paper to confirm that I will be working at the McD's at the Owen Drive Location. "You're hard to work with, William," She said sternly. I didn't care. The last 10 months (Oct 1994-July 1995), that I was an employee at McD's was very combative. I was going through some tough times. I had no one to talk to. I was getting worse. I was in a War Zone. The employees knew that I was difficult to work with. I should've just quit. I was applying to attend Winston-Salem University in which Mr Williams didn't want me to go there. He warned me. Like, Yoda and Obi-Wan Kenobi warned Luke Skywalker not to confront Darth Vader until he was fully trained as a Jedi Knight. But, Luke, He had to learn the hard the way. And a Shocking Truth.

Working at the McD's at Owen Drive was nothing but chaos and turmoil. They took no mercy on me. I had to work in the Grill area, Fri-Tue at 5am-1pm. Working on weekends. DAMN! But I had to do it. I felt Miserable. I Hated Working at McD's. I Hated it. I HATED IT.

I was the subject of rumors. CRAZY. LOONEY. STALKER. I was in a negative environment. I got into constant arguments. I wasn't getting along with anybody. I had a real Bad Attitude. I wasn't the only one. There were lots characters at that store. But, I was the VILLAIN. I was constantly up and very very exhausted. So, I planned a vacation for next summer to Attend the Clifford Brown Jazz Festival in Wilmington, Delaware. The Personal Clifford Benjamin Brown (1930-1956), was an American Jazz Musician who played the Trumpet, in the early 1950's. His life was cut short by a car accident on June 26, 1956. He was not only involved in the accident. His bandmate, pianist, Richie Powell and wife Nancy, who was inexperienced in driving the car on the rain slicked streets by the Pennsylvania Turnpike. Clifford Brown was only 25. He was just a Boy. The World of Jazz, lost perhaps and arguably the Best Trumpeter in Jazz along with Fats Navarro.

I highly appreciated Clifford Brown. I loved the Man. But there would one be a Two-word Question, "What if?"

But I had to deal with those Imbeciles at McD's. I was just in a World of Negativity. It was unorganized. Believe me. There were Kids quitting. There were times the Grill would break down and it needed maintenance. Janet just put me there to deal with all that drama there. I strongly feel it was planned to have me transferred all along. They were just waiting for right time. But having me transferred didn't make things better at the Bragg Blvd Location. It only got worse. Nothing changed. But it wasn't my problem anymore.

The most of the employees were very ignorant. The McD's location on Owen Drive was very rural. I had to tolerate them. I knew that I wasn't going to work there too long. That wasn't my life. I wanted something Better in my life.

My mood Swings was really unpredictable. There were times, I was being very likable guy at 24 years old. But then I was just a "Monster". The Supervisor Kristy and the others were trying figure me out. I was flirting with the girls but this time. It would be my last.

I must share a few stories when I was working there. They're not good. I'm not making any of my co-workers Famous. I was in a World of Negativity. The Distress, Anguish and Stigma, I endure those last months working at McD's.

As I was working, I was still the Crew trainer. Working hard as ever, of course there were gossip and rumors. Mostly females. Anyway, As I was transferred, They needed help in the grill Area. That was the main reason I was transferred there. I was one of the two who could operate and run the grill area. But they just wanted me for the weekends and I hated it. An elderly lady, Aretha, who has been working for a long time. And she had seniority there and she was highly respected. Things went her way and I had to go along with the program. I was a new employee there. In the evening, Kids from South View High School worked. They didn't want to work morning shift. They really didn't do any work.

But trouble was brewing. There was a girl, Danielle who was pregnant. She was all loud. Talkative. I just dealt with her. One day, When my shift was over, I cleaned up the Grill area and I had to mop the floor. Somehow accidently, she slipped and fell on the floor. She, all of sudden accused of doing that purpose when I was mopping the floor. I think she was overacting. So, one day, Her Boyfriend, A Black guy who keep looking at me. He was in the lobby and he wanted to talk to me. As a Man, I walked to him. He told me that I was the cause of her getting hurt. I told him I didn't do anything to her. He was still mad and told me, "Look after her for me alright?" I just looked at him and I went back to the Grill area. That Bitch lied on me. As I mopped on the floor, She just slipped. It wasn't intentional. I had to leave her alone. This white girl was always flirting with me and a few other guys. Making guys touch her pregnant stomach. She was a making jokes who was the "Baby's Daddy". I guess since I was a new employee. She had every advantage. I never talked to her.

There was another Female who was the cashier giving me Hell. We always argued. We just didn't get along at all. Yes, Edna tried to talk to me. Everybody at that store knew about us bickering. I stayed away from her as much as I could. She made me highly uncomfortable. The maintenance Man, Martin, A big burly guy, Who I remembered I attended Terry Sanford with made jokes on Edna and I. A few girls told me that she had a crush on me. I didn't like Edna. She had a real negative attitude.

Lastly, a girl, Monica, who had gotten me into serious trouble. It was her word against mine. Yes, I flirted with her as well. Let me point that out. One day in the afternoon, after my shift, I asked for her number. She gave it to me. I was calling her from time to time. We talked about what was going on at the job and she asked me about my situation with Danielle's Boyfriend. I told her it was nothing. We both worked the same shift. I would take her home. I guess it was no problem. She was a single mother and she showed a picture of her child. Now this was almost during the Holidays.

Christmas was approaching. I was Depressed. Very Depressed. I had to deal with the Constant drama at McD's. It was very tough for me. No one knew that I deeply troubled and highly irritable. Even, Mr Williams couldn't help me. I was still practicing my Guitar. I was excited contacting "Chick" who was a highly appreciator of Clifford Brown. He lived in Wilmington, Delaware and he organized The Clifford Brown Jazz Festival. A very kind man. Highly respected and his family were good-hearted. I needed a Vacation. Definitely. Most Definitely. So, I planned to travel to Delaware the next summer. I couldn't wait. I couldn't drive there But I had to take a Train, My travel agent, Jeanine Bergman told me.

I was feeling low and worthless. But I kept my head up and moved on. I called Monica. I left messages. And I noticed she never returned my phone calls. Things wasn't going right for me. One night, I went to a strip club called the Doll House and I befriended a Bouncer named, Berry. Big huge Guy. He was a pool Hustler and he kind of looked out for me. I was a regular at the club. The Girls were good on stage but had nasty attitudes. I will say this; Those girls needed to go to a Mental Institution, seriously. Those girls had issues. That night during the Christmas Holidays, I was at the club. Berry sensed that I was down and out. He was looked at me that night. He spoke kindly to me. I didn't order a drink. "Are you Okay, Man?" He tried to cheer me up. I couldn't hardly say a word. I was rambling terribly to myself. I was pitiful.

I tried to reach out a few people. No one came to me. Christmas Eve, I went to Midnight mass at St Ann Church. But it didn't make me feel any better. Christmas came and went.

1995. A New Year. And????? Nothing changed. My niece and Nephew had their wonderful Christmas. Now at the Doomed McD's, I was the labeled, "STALKER". I didn't know what was going on. But it has to do with Monica. January, One night, this was daylight savings time. I called her up and we talked. Then, she suggested that I should come to her apartment so that we could talk. So, it was no Big deal as I observed. It was around 5:45-7:00pm. I went on impulse and I got ready to go. Now, let me point this out to you. I had no intention. No intention whatsoever of trying to attack her. I drove to her apartment, It was pitch Black that night. I arrived at her apartment. I got out of my GEO-METRO, I went to the door and knocked on her door a few times. I waited for her open the door and then I knocked on her window. Then suddenly, I heard this small scream, 'WHAT IS IT??". It was her. So, I got back in my Car and left. That's what happened.

That shit wasn't over at all. No way. The episode reached tp McD's on Owen Drive. Just about everyone heard what took place. But, the blame was put on me. Monica told everybody there that I came by her apartment at 12midnight, 1am. That I was kicking and baming on her door. THAT WAS A LIE. One of the girls, Carol, wanted to talk to me about what happened. I explained what happened. I had to defend myself. I said that I came to her apartment. I knocked on the door. And I left. It was around, 6:00pm-7:00pm. Not 12am or 1am in the morning. Thus, Monica's friend, Carol told me to leave her alone and that she was uncomfortable talking to me. I had no one to turn to. McDonald's Owen Drive Employees was against me. I felt like I was going to be crucified. Along with my arguments with Edna fueled. It was a Gossip Filled, Persecution and Ignorant War against me. Hell, even the managers knew about it. It was Monica's Word was against mine. I knew would have been fired and went to Jail.

I HEARD YOU WAS CRAZY! YOU STALK GIRLS! CRAZY ASS!

I couldn't do nothing. I was under the table. I was about to cause a riot. Or being chased out and be stoned to death. Lynched. Monica continued to spread those rumors and lies about me.

Edna and I still carried on our arguments. As everybody was shaking their heads. One day, I was about to clock out from work. The tensions between us was raising high. I walked out to my car in the parking lot. Edna was outside with Aretha and another lady. All of a sudden, Out in the Parking lot. Edna was yelling and screaming, "YOU A STUPID MUTHA FUCKA!!! A CRAZY MUTHA FUCKA!! It's a good thing that I didn't Retaliate. I said, "You're stupid." As I got in my car and Left.

The next Day, News of the Verbal Altercation between Edna and I spreaded like Wild fire. Olivia, a Swing manager, who was my age, walked straight to me. "What was that argument between you and Edna all about?" I told her my side of the story. She just walked away and shook her head. But this was getting ridiculous, indeed. It was like everybody was POINTING THEIR FINGER AT ME!! There was no one I could turn to. RUMORS. GOSSIP. I had a growing Blind Hatred for Monica and Edna. Oh, I had to help them out on the Grill area. Life of the Party. All of that drama hurt me deeply inside.

I was so surprised that I didn't SNAP! I kept my cool. I was the VILLAIN. THE PREDATOR. NORMAN BATES. I was really wearing down. Much to my surprise, I got accepted to Winston-Salem University. Yeah Great! That Spring, I was getting ready for my trip to Wilmington, Delaware. The Clifford Brown Jazz Festival. During Easter Sunday, I had to work. I was pissed as Hell. Because it was dead. It wasn't busy. I worked 5am-12pm. It really established my disdain working at McD's. I continued going through my mood swings. During this time, I wasn't getting any sleep from time to time. I was just chasing people away because of my behavior. Aretha was really aware that I was easily disturbed. My friction with Edna continued. If she had a crush on me, that's her. She was very rude towards not only me but a few employees. I didn't learn later that incident at the parking lot that everyone, Especially the owners knew all about what happened. I was surprised that Edna didn't get fired because she was very loud cursing me out in front of the customers. But she got away with it. I was feeling paranoid and I had to look after myself. I knew that my time and days working at McD's were numbered.

Then, Kristy had a talk with me. I told her a little bit about myself. She asked me about my troubles. I told her about the "rumors' about me. She told me about her experience with her ex-husband. He verbally abused her. But she told me not to let words or comments bother me. I needed a Vacation.

June 1995. I just turned 25. I was excited to go to Wilmington, Delaware. So, I purchased my Train Tickets and my Hotel reservation. I was going to meet "Chick". Dad was worried about me going there But I knew the night before, My Dad called him or either "Chick" Called him. So, that Midnight, Dad had to drop me off at the AMTRAK train station in downtown Fayetteville. I was ready to leave. But the issue was I didn't get any sleep during my ride on my Train. It stopped to other stations. Especially in Virginia. I dozed off. And the train stopped at Washington DC. I was there for 3-4 hours. But I was excited to see the US. Capitol. I was in a different world. I was feeling the same way as I traveled to California, four years earlier. Soon, I finally arrived in Wilmington Delaware, the Birthplace of Clifford Brown. I arrived at the Station as "Chick" came. A very friendly man. Big and Chubby, He had a Big Smile on his Face. Wearing an African Dashiki and some nice Beige Khakis. It was a Warm Greeting, indeed. I got my luggage. I got into his car. He had a deep gruff Voice. A Delaware accent. A large Face with a big Beard. Sort of a Santa Clause. I told that I have to call my mother to tell her I was okay. He spoke to my mother on the phone. So, the plan was He dropped me off to my hotel to check in, which it wasn't very nice. The room smelled like Smoke. It seems the people who were there before me smoked a lot. I only stayed there for one day. So, Chick took me to another hotel. It was more clean. More sanitary.

I certainly enjoyed myself. My Mood swing was High. Overly Excited just as I was when I was at California. I met Chick's His Lovely Wife and his Son, "Hot Rod". Chick was a very sociable and gregarious man. I had nothing but respect for him. The festival was free. It was held at Rodney Square in downtown Wilmington. It was a different environment for me. It was a very Fast City not Laid back and slow Compared to Fayetteville. Wilmington, Delaware was very busy. A Jazz City dedicated a Festival to it's favorite son. I was introduced to The Family of Clifford Brown the first night of the festival. His two surviving sisters and his Brother Leon, He was a Character. I met his Widow, LaRue Brown Watson, perhaps the one of the most kindest person I ever met. I was very excited. "Chick" wanted me to feel really welcomed to him and his Family. A highly educated Man. I loved his Wild "sense of humor". The next day, He took me a tour of Wilmington. Clifford Brown's house, the highschool he attended. But Jazz is the language in Wilmington, Delaware. Especially if you play trumpet. But there was one thing that "Chick" knew that I loved the Ray Noble tune, "Cherokee". A beautiful tune. It was the first tune, I heard played by Clifford "Brownie" Brown. Brownie was a Powerhouse Trumpet Player. WHY DID HE HAVE TO DIE SO F@#ing Young???? I was talking to one of his cousins and she told me that He was talking to her the Day before his death saying he wasn't feeling right and he knew something terrible was going to happen. I felt more relaxed and calm. Then one Day, "Chick' and I took to riding . We talked about things. He sensed there was something was annoying me and Irritating me because I telling about my Hatred of working at McD's. He calmed me down and he knew that I was under stress of some kind. But I didn't come to Wilmington, Delaware just let Chick Hear me ranting and raving about my personal problems. I was there to have a good time. I took lots of photos when I was there. In honoring, the late Clifford Brown, there was always events in clubs around Wilmington. If you play an instrument? You can join in. I think that's the meaning of Jazz; doing your own thing. For me, what was also special was getting acquainted with LaRue, She was very understanding and Kind. I asked her all sorts of questions about her relationship to Brownie. But it was all good. She knew that I loved her Husband and his music. LaRue was coordinator of the Clifford Brown Jazz Foundation with her son, Clifford Brown Jr.

'Oh, I remember Clifford.'

Well, unfortunately, time flies when you're having fun. I had to return home. Getting back into the swing of things. Fayetteville, NC. Backwards Fayetteville, NC. Yes, I can point that out because I live there. All that I can say Fayetteville is a growing town. Enough Said.

I promised Chick that I will see him again. I had to prepare myself to go to School. Chick stressed the importance of getting an education. A friend of Chick took me back to the AMTRAK station that Sunday afternoon. Chick had business to take care of. It was time for me to leave. I had to go home.

I returned to work. Same'ol. Same'ol. I was trying to contain myself. Still, I was irritable And I wanted to Walk out of my Job. But I gave my notice that I will be resigning. Quitting McD's for good. I had other things to focus on. I didn't want to be around People who were negative and cruel. I wanted a positive atmosphere. I wasn't perfect. I was already labled as a STALKER. CRAZY. That didn't go away. Ever.

As I returned to work. My Family was getting ready to move away from 734 Eufaula Street that summer. Leaving the BOTTOM! Because there was a Dump site behind our neighborhood. It was beginning to smell bad because of the Hot Weather. We were having problems with pests too in our house. Roaches and Mice were in our house for the past several years. I was getting sick of it. So, people from our neighborhood protested that we need to leave because of the pests. My parents looked for another house. We were supposed to move back in '81 but I think it was either my Father or mother decided to stay. They looked at houses in area near where my father worked. And I would have attended Pine Forest Senior High. I think that would've been a different experience?? I don't know. My behavior was highly Manic. No, It wouldn't be different. So, My Parents found a Two-Story house in Hillendale North.

At the end of July, We were preparing to move. My last month working at McD's was coming to an end.

I had to get ready for School at Winston-Salem State University. I wanted to major in Music. I wanted to play Guitar. I really didn't have a Classical Guitar. My instructor was Mr Matthis. I spoke to him over the phone numerous times. But I had to audition before the Music Faculty. THAT I DIDN'T KNOW. Well, I went to the Summer Orientation that July. I must be Honest, I did have a chip on my Shoulder. I had to learn the hard way. I insulted one of the music instructors there. That wasn't good. I thought I knew about Music But I was definitely musically illiterate. Mr Williams warned me. But I thought I had it in the Bag. I didn't audition before the Faculty. NO. NO. I didn't. I had enough Balls to offend the Band Director about playing Drums for the Band. I didn't even play drums in AGES!!!! I had to disrespect Mr Jackson. I was only a member of his Band for 5 minutes. The percussion section was looking at me with the expression. "Who's this Guy? "Who's this Fool?" Then I quit and I have to apologize to him. This was not what I had expected.

I stayed at Wilson Hall. One of the Best dormitories on the Campus. And you have to achieve a certain Grade Point average to stay there. I was only there for that weekend. But the one thing that I love was the City of Winston-Salem. Blue and Green that's all I could tell you. A Beautiful City. I had trouble coming home. I was all over I40-West for 3-4 hours, I was driving all over the Piedmont and I almost was going to Tennessee. Because, I had to go to I40-East to return to Fayetteville. It was an exhausting day for me. I finally had to reach to Greensboro to get back 421 South to Sanford and back to Fayetteville.

I was getting ready to leave McD's. But, My Co-workers didn't want me to go. Of all that Friction, Constant Arguments and Rumors, I had to endure. Stigma and hardships. It was time for me to leave. I went on impulse to leave. I got my belongings together of what I need. But still, I had this knowledge of music that I didn't have. Again, Mr

Williams didn't want me to go. As I pointed out, I had to learn the hard way. Just as, Luke Skywalker wanted to save his Friends and confront Darth Vader when Yoda and Obi-Wan Kenobi told him not to go to Bespin.

That last Saturday of July, I was gone but McD's from Owen Drive called me to come to work. NO! I'm done with McDonald's. I returned only to get my last paycheck. My Family had moved to a new house in Hillendale North. Well, that second week of August, I left to go for WSSU. My mother told me one thing and it stuck in my brain to this day, "Reap what you sow." I had to stay at Brown Hall, The only Boys dorm, that August Sunday was hot. My Dad and Tonya arrived. It was crowded. I was assigned to the second Floor. The next Day, I had to register for Classes. My roommate was from Virginia and he moved in later that Day. His name was Tommy. Since our rooms were Hot. I had my Fan and I tried to make my stay as comfortable as possible. When it was time for my Family to leave, We said our Goodbyes and I almost got emotional. All the new students got all sociable. My roommate and I got acquainted. It was okay. But we later would have disagreements. There were few of students from Fayetteville. I recognize, a girl that worked at McD's. She never talked to me. I didn't waste my time trying talking to her. That whole night, all I heard was Hip-Hop music all through the hall. It didn't bother me.

Yes, I was a little bothered for being 25 years old but there were few guys that were in their early 20's too. I kept that a secret. Some knew that I was older by the way I talked. But, I couldn't waste no time because I had to register for classes if not I would have to move out.

Now, this is a historically Black College since 1892. They had a great Music Program. And Nursing program. That institution of education for the African-American Youth was growing and expanding. Enter to learn. Depart to serve.

I didn't know that registering class was so stressful for me. I was up, down and all around the Campus. I wasn't the only one. That week in August was scorching Hot. I went to the Fine Arts

Department. I talked to Dr Anderson, Who told me that I supposed to have auditioned last month. I wasn't part of the Music Program. Mr Matthis told me he was going to be my Guitar instructor. No. No No. I was supposed audition before the Faculty. I had to do it that week. I didn't know what to do. I couldn't reach out to him. Well, I got into a squabble with the choir Director Mrs Carson. I tried for the choir. I came to her office and I sung a verse to "Lift every Voice and Sing". She said that my voice was Alto range. She was very demanding and harsh. She told me that I had today to audition. Well, I had no choice. So, that scorching hot Afternoon. I was already angry at her being demanding. So, Iater that afternoon, I had to audition before the music Faculty. I had an attitude, Yes. I was miserable. Dr Anderson had told me, 'Play what you know."

My Guitar that I had was a piece of junk. It wasn't even a Classical Guitar. The strings were rusty and I was out of tune. I attempted to play, Tchaikovsky's Arabian dance in D major and Leo Brouwer Etude No. 6. I was out of position in playing the Damn thing. I was out of rhythm. I gave them my all. When they questioned me about how much I knew about music. I knew nothing. But there was hope for me. A soft, short, diminutive woman was rooting for me. She was the piano instructor. Fair-skinned complexioned with a kind demeanor. Little did I know, I was going to see more of her later. Well, when it was over. I knew I was unprepared. But it wasn't over. I left that building in disgrace. Again, it wasn't over for me yet.

I had to finish registering for my classes. And my name wasn't on the computer file. I was so frustrated. A few guys were laughing because I waited to the last minute. So, A kind man, Mr Lovett helped me get my situation straight and he found out that I was a remedial Student. He went to his computer and he asked me about my audition and I answered, "Well I-" "You in there. Don't worry about it, You in there." He interrupted. I tried to answer him. He replied, "Look we ain't no NC School of the Arts." So, Mr Lovett had my classes registered and I was in the clear.

Of all that stress I was going through that day, I thought things was going to get better for me But it didn't. Not by a long shot.

The next day, I was called to the Fine Arts. Bad News. I was given a letter by the Chair person. I wasn't accepted in the Music Department by my horrible performance before the Faculty. I knew that they were going to get me. "Do you have anything to say?" Actually, I had nothing to say was my little friction with the choir director, Mrs Carson, I didn't appreciate how rude to me she was. I lost already. I had nobody to turn to. I had to take some classes required by the Music Faculty. Music Theory I, Piano Minor I, Sight Reading I. Of course, I had my lessons with Mr Matthis. He knew about my audition also. Again, It was like I committed the crime of the Century. I was the rejected Student. I was really hurt. All that stress I went through the week before And I had nobody to turn to. But I have the Spring Semester to audition. Mr Matthis, I must be honest, was no help for me at all. He was a guitar instructor at this Pearson's Music on Peter's Creek Parkway. And he was the chairman of the Piedmont Guitar Society in Greensboro. He just had a lot to do. He just didn't have anytime for me. He was completely useless.

So, one day at the Fine Arts Department, the little woman who was present at my horrible audition. I felt ashamed and embarrassed. "TRAVIS!!" Mrs Clara Fields caught me in the hallway. She told me that will be in Piano Minor I. And she will be teaching me. Then the other instructor Dr Henson would be my adviser. He helped me out a lot. We would chat in his office. And he would teach me Music Theory I. Through that Fall Semester, I had a lot of Work to do. No lie. I was thinking being away from Fayetteville it would make me feel better but it didn't. My Mood Swings was Up and down. Highly impulsive. A few students noticed my behavior. Especially, when I took a Part Time Job working at the Radio Station WSSU 90.5. They play only Jazz. I was very quiet and so anxious that I was wondering around. I had some frictions with the Students. Since being there at WSSU, I was falling, falling and falling. I was really declining.

I started my Piano Minor I, with Mrs Fields. I had a lot to prove to her and the Faculty that I can play Music. So, I started learning how to play the piano. I was the only student that's learning to play the Guitar and it was like everyone was looking up to me. I just had a lot to do. Back at my Dorm. Boys will be Boys. You can hear the Blasts of Hip-Hop Artists in Rooms and old School Soul Music. And yes, the Fumigated Marijuana. The Boys Blazing (Smoking, I mean). There were Fraternities and Sororities. There were Dance parties. I must say, that attending a Black College made me proud. I can't complain. I made a few acquaintances. The Students there were not Bad. Some were arrogant if you're not part of a Clique. I was just myself. The Boys in my Floor talked about the 7-digit numbers that they got from the Girls. Yes, I got a few too. I was "Searching" and I had fun going to the Football Games. The Marching Band was Okay But it was nothing like NCA&T in Greensboro. Fights would break out with Fraternities. Real Stupid Stuff. I must say that I was never bored being there. Never. There was always something for me to do.

I got straight to my practicing my Guitar and in truth, I was getting nowhere. When Autumn arrived, Mr Mathis contracted a Cold and some of the lessons were canceled. The City, Winston-Salem was Beautiful in autumn. The Fall leaf colors, Red, Yellow and orange. It was like I was in a different world. But still, I was homesick. I would return home for the weekend. My mother told me that why won't I stay at Winston-Salem than just coming home every weekend. She was right.

At school, I stayed and I was having arguments with my roommate, Tommy. Partly, it had to do with my playing the Guitar. It bothered him a lot. He stayed out late. His TV would be on and I would have to cut it off. We really didn't have a plan. At times, I tried to talk to him. But he would get defensive. Sometimes Girls would call him and his phone would ring all the time. Whenever I had homework and study, I did it.

So, I befriended a kid at my Biology Class. He was a Cool Guy and we hit it off. He would joke with me about my voice. That I had a "voice from the Radio". He knew I had talent. His name was Lester. He was from Winston-Salem and he knew a lot about Hip-Hop. I would take him home. He stayed off campus. He stayed at Skyline. A pretty tough neighborhood. I had to watch myself.

Lester was a real laid back Guy. A lean, Dark-complexioned, He was handsome in a delicate way. He sported a light mustache and a Goatee. He resembled Eddie Kendricks of the Temptations. He kept very much to himself. Whenever the Class was over he would look at the Girls. One Girl who he spotted was in my Mathematics Class. "Now, She's correct," He commented on her. We really got along really well. I was surprised that he would always come to me in class. He was smart. Me, I was trying to do the best I could. Biology Class was very interesting. In the Lab, The Teacher, was Mrs Johnson, but she was very Fond of Lester. Mrs Johnson was a short little middle aged woman with brown hair and a high-pitched voice. She was very helpful. So, one day, After Class, He wanted me to come to his place and hang out. I didn't want to hang out the kids. All the Guys did in dorm was smoke weed, get drunk, inviting girls over. Whenever I go to the Bathroom I see a few condoms scattered in and around the toilet or vomit from someone who can't handle beer or liquor. Boys slamming doors hard in the middle of night when everyone's sleeping that's what made that Dorm terrible. I just had to deal with it. And the Girl's dorm, Atkins Hall was just as worse from what I heard.

Back then, people had pagers not cell phones yet. So, I would call Lester on the pay phone or my room mates phone. I would come to his apartment. I had to be careful because he had a Rotwieler and puppy Pit Bull. I met his girlfriend, Felicia and he had a few Kids. She already knew me because Lester told her all about me. He had a good taste in music, Hip-Hop Especially and 'ol School Soul Music. I commented him, "Lester, you're a very open-minded". He replied kindly, "Cause, I'm a very open-minded guy". But one thing we both had in common we were Dallas Cowboys Fans. Lester was tough. And he knew how to handle himself. I was around the tough section of Winston-Salem. I socialized with his "Boys". It was no problem. They were Cool. I hang out and I dranked a few beers. His people really got a "KicK" out of me. Especially his cousin, Darryl. One time as I was talking to Lester and I referred myself as a "Human Being".

One Friday Night after a party at his apartment with his Friends, Lester wanted to talk to me. Took a ride in his car late that night. It was cold and chilly. As he drove as he drove almost out of Winston-Salem on I-40, he started the conversation. "Are you confused about your sexuality?" That question came to me as a complete shock. I never thought he'd ask me anything like that. I was confused. A little lost. And I answered softly, "No". "Have you been molested? "No", I replied. "Are you a Virgin? Have you ever got some pussy?" If you didn't, you're a man, It ain't nothing wrong, Man. You have all these people with AIDS and all that shit." I was so confused. Lester talked as I listened. He just talked to me about Life. He told me more about himself. I didn't know where he was getting at. As he returned to his apartment, he told me one thing and I was marveled as we both got out of his car, "You're Special."

Now, I returned to campus. I was thinking to myself. Why was this guy I hardly knew asking me questions like that? It really sunked into my Head. It bothered me but I was sensing he was trying to point out that I had a problems. The symptoms of my Manic Behavior and being Impulsive was being noticed. Yes, it did Bothered me But He was telling me everything was going to be alright with me. I guess he was trying to tell me to look at myself.

Anyway, I was at the School. Tensions with my roommate, Tommy was rising. I just couldn't talk to the guy. But I was trying to reach out to him, He would walk away. I knew practicing my Guitar was bothering him. He was always staying out late. I couldn't socialize with his Friends. They were just 'Wanna Be Thugs". I don't understand why do you have to be a "Thug" to be accepted? The Young African-American Men just need to learn to be themselves. Quit being something you're not. I wasn't raised that way. If I was trying to be a "Thug", "Hustler" or a "Knucklehead". I wouldn't last a day. Or a week for that matter. Enough said on that subject.

Now, Back to School, I was attending Classes and doing my best. And from time to time, Getting acquainted with the "Sistas" at a Black College. Be down with the "Beautiful Woman". What a Laugh. I'm not going to spend or waste my time on that subject either.

As time was going by, I was having some problems with the students in my music classes. Yes, I was defensive at a Few of them.

Asking me my age. Most of all, How long I played my Guitar. And the Drama with the School Band and disrespecting the Band Director. That wasn't good. I was called a "Sell out".

You see, I'm one of those "Different Blacks" you can't figure out. The way you talk and how you carry yourself. RETARDED. CRAZY. WHERE YOU FROM? WHY YOU TALK THE WAY YOU TALK? I CAN'T FIGURE YOU OUT! YOU JUST CRAZY!! THAT BOY'S WEIRD OVER THERE. OH, HE JUST MAKES SICK!! I CAN'T STAND HIM!! I HATE HIM!!! DAMN CRAZY!!

I was progressing on my Piano Minor I, Mrs Fields could see that. She, also could see that I was strained. Easily disturbed. Edgy. Something was really Bothering me. Some of the Students was seeing it.

I had a new roommate, Oscar. Tommy decided to move out. We just weren't getting along. Oscar came along. He was majoring in Physical Therapy. He was okay. I had no issues with him but he was having his own problems too. He was being Bullied by his ex-roommate. A "Wanna be Thug". As we were getting acquainted. He was quiet. He did his school work. And I had an altercation with his ex-roommate. I was so Angry. I called Lester. And he knew that I was so full of rage as I was talking to him on the phone. He was calm He told me to come over his place. Then Oscar's ex-roommate was kicking the door. Oscar was quiet. He didn't do nothing but that was his problem. He should've confronted him. But Tommy (my ex-roommate) was giving me problems. A girl who he was talking to was trying to give me trouble. So, one night, I approached to Tommy, He was high smoking Weed and I told him about what was going on. I told him to warn her to stop trying to harass me. He look like he didn't want to be bothered with me. Like a Man, I told him the crap is going to stop. The Girl stopped bothering me.

The stress was really Irkking me. Now, I came to Lester's apartment. I was shaking and his Boys were bugging off of me. They told me to "Chill and relax". I explained to him what happened. And He told me he and his Boys would be on "the News" if they were to go to my dorm. He asked his girlfriend Felicia on what he would do. She nodded her head to me. "We get down, Dawg!", He said simply.

November- It was towards the end of the Fall Semester. I was really worried about what was going on. My studies. That Failed Audition. It was No way over for me. So, during the Thanksgiving Holidays, I came home. Now, I went to the Flea Market and purchased a golden Brass Knuckles and a Switch-Blade. I didn't know what I was thinking about. But I needed to protect myself. Little did I know I was headed for Trouble returning to WSSU.

Piano Minor I Class. I was doing real good. Because I had a little YAMAHA keyboard Mr Williams gave me. I used it a lot, learning Scales. Chords. Playing easy exercises in the piano book. Mrs Fields was getting more proud of me as I was making much progress. Since, I was learning to play the Classical Guitar with Mr Matthis. In truth, I was getting no where. He would just give me a few pieces or some I chose. I was struggling. And my Second Audition was approaching for the New Year.

Sadly enough, I was impulsive, getting agitated and easily irritable. There was a student in my Music Theory I and Piano class. "JC" was always asking about my playing guitar. He was member of the Band. Okay? He played Drums. I didn't like the Kid anyway. I must be honest, I was snappy towards him at one time and a few other Students. He was bullying me and I didn't have time for that. I think He just wanted to take his frustrations or his problems out on me. He knew that I was soft and edgy.

One day in December, I went to my Piano Minor I class. I was waiting in the hall outside of Class, the same kid in my music theory class, my class named "JC" he walked out of the Bathroom as he walking towards me He asked roughly, "How old are you, Man?" I fired back at him, "Why you wanna know?" The tensions between "JC" and I was boiling. "I just asked you a question!", Then He tried slap me but somehow He hit my cap as he was getting ready to fight me. Suddenly, I pulled out my Golden Brass Knuckles. "Oh So Wassup? You got those Brass knuckles, FUCK YOU, Man!" And I snapped back "FUCK YOU, Too Bitch!", I said defensively.

Then "JC" walked out the Lobby. I could hear his voice. Ranting and Raving about what I done to him. He was loud. "I ain't going down like that, NAHHHH MAN!." So, I went to the Classroom and waited for Mrs Fields to show up. So, I was sitting down. That Punk comes in the class with two Boys. One of the guys was a Fraternity member. And they threatened me. "Why you pull out your Brass Knuckles on me, Man??? I was only trying to talk to you, Man!!!" The Frat member joined in. "He was only trying to talk to you!" I was in a corner and I really had nothing to say. I was scared and I looked at them as they continued their threats. "I'll Kill you, Bitch, I'll Kill you Bitch. I got people everywhere! I'll Kill you, Bitch!!. So, the Frat member Threaten me, "If you do that again, I'll Fuck you up. I'll fuck you up! Understand?? You have a Good Day." As He left, the "JC" was still going off, "You really piss me off. You really piss me off!" as he walked out of the room.

I was terrified. Angered. There was nothing I could do. I was shaking. I just wished I could go out there in that hallway and beat him unmercifully. My emotions was bottling up. So, as "JC" and another student came to class. I just sat there in my seat. Mrs Fields knew that I was very upset and my head was down. I told her that I wanted to talk to her. "Can it be after class?", she asked. I answered, "Yes." Piano Minor I began. I sat there at my piano. I didn't touch nothing. That Creep who tried to pick a fight with me was being all innocent and being nice to Mrs Fields. But still, my head was down. When class was over as the students left. Mrs Fields was out in the Hallway.

As, Mrs Fields returned to class, She rushed to me, with Her voice was pleading, "Travis, Travis, What's the matter? Are you okay?" As she said that I burst with tears and I wept uncontrollably as my head was still down. I couldn't speak. I barely muttered words to her. She asked me about what happened and I told her."If you're not happy here then I'm sorry, " She said as she was comforting me. She asked me gently, "Was it, JC?" I nodded my head. I continued to weep and weep. So, Mrs Fields had helped me to play an exercise on the piano. She was so gentle and patient. Slowly I played the piece. It was really kind of her to do that. She was reaching out to me. After we finished that I got my books and I followed her to her office. I explained everything to her what happened and everything that happened prior to that awful audition. I gave her those Brass Knuckles. Still, recovery from my grief. She thanked me for sharing that with her.

Buying that switch-blade and those Brass Knuckles, I wasn't accomplishing anything. It was like If I purchased a Gun, I would surely be asking for trouble. I'm not a Thug or a Hustler. I wasn't raised that way. I was only looking out for myself after my confrontation with Oscar's Stupid Wanna-Be Thug ex-roommate.

I went to see Lester, immediately. He was putting up decorations on his Christmas tree. I was in impulsive and manic. He already knew that I was bothered by something. His cousin Darryl was there as we were talking. I liked Lester's cousin. A cool kid. I acted like that incident with that kid in piano class was no Big Deal. Lester, was hearing me talking about doing something. "You better not let that shit get to you. It's going to go all in your Head." I even gave his cousin that switch-blade. "I like that, Man" as Darryl looked at it. I was at Lester's place that whole evening until it got pitch Black Dark. Lester knew that incident with that kid, still bothered me. "That Boy had no right touching or putting his hand on you. Those Frat Boys come over here, they're going get it." He lectured me as I was started crying again. "Gone and cry Man." He knew that I needed someone to talk to. "You're different and I don't know you but you letting that shit mess up your Head." Again, He was eluding that I needed help.

I felt I was losing. Just losing. At a College when Mr Williams told me not to go. And having the audacity to tell that Music Faculty what I want and don't want was Foul. It was hitting me. Yet, again, it was not over for me.

Dec-1995 I was so worried about my classes I didn't know if I was going pass or not. I couldn't wait for the Christmas Break. So, I came home. I was home for the whole month and the first week of January. But I was impulsive. I got into an argument with my Dad and Tonya in our new den in our new home. My moodiness was evidently going awry. I was just Highly Manic. I wasn't thinking straight. One of my friends from St Ann School called me one night. Willie just recently broke up with his girlfriend. He was depressed but I just listened. He was my friend. My childhood chum. I was there for him. I spoked to him over for 3 hours. Breaking up with your Girlfriend during the Christmas Holidays. Very Bad.

So, I went over to his house to visit him for a minutes just to check up on him. I was there for him. He needed someone to lean on. That's how I am.

Later that night, I went to Thee Doll House to look for a Girl (Stripper), I knew But I was told she no longer works there. I was disappointed. I didn't stay there long, I returned home.

Christmas-1995 came and went. But it was mostly for my nephew and niece of course. They got a lot toys. I was thinking about a Girl I met at school. Only to be rejected when I returned in January. But, I was hardly getting any sleep. My mood swings was on and off. A Rollercoaster. But I was very very tired. I went to Paradise Records and Tapes. I already bought, THE BEATLES ANTHOLOGY VOL. I. So I purchased, "To Be Continued" CD by Issac Hayes. It contains the sample of his rendition of the Burt Bachrach classic "The Look of Love." I had my Nice Fisher Stereo Cassette/CD Player in Addition to that I had my first Portable CD player. I love Music. I LOVE MUSIC. I LOVE MUSIC.

January 1996. Fayetteville was receiving harsh wintry weather over the holidays. A Bad Ice Storm and the whole State of NC was under downtime. I was getting worried about the weather in Winston-Salem because I had to drive back to the Piedmont terrain Which received A huge amount of Snow. So, I had to be very very careful Behind the Wheel of my 1992 GEO-METRO XFI. My Stick Ride. The road was covered in Black Ice when it became dark. The Temperatures was dropping when I was driving through Guiford/ Forsythe County. Very Cold. But I returned to school safely.

My Dorm, Brown Hall was Cold. Winston-Salem got hit hard during that winter storm. My room was so cold. I was hoping the heater or whatever you want to call it wasn't working at all. Unfortunately, I wasn't getting any rest for that matter. I was so impulsive that I wasn't thinking most of the time. Irritable. And it was time for my Second Audition for the Music Faculty. I was still worried about that. I was practicing my Guitar. So, I selected two pieces from an Aaron Shearer book and that was it. But those Music Instructors were ready and waiting for me. Mrs Fields was trying to contact Mr Mathis to confirm my next Audition was going to take place. But he was going to be there.

The Second Audition was on the second week of January. The whole Faculty was there. Yes, even Mr Mathis. I was more confident that I was. I was still nervous. I tried my best But it was much better than the First that previous summer in August. I had my White Dress shirt, My tie, Black dress pants and shoes. I gave my all. Mrs Fields and Dr Henson spoke up for me. And all the Faculty were respectable. More attentive. I played my two pieces. I felt a great burden on me doing it. When, I finished, Mr Matthis roared with an applause for everyone. I had to play two piano pieces Mrs Fields selected for me. I did that fine. I was asked a few questions to test my Music Theory. Overall, It was okay. At the end of the audition, I had to Apologize to the Faculty in Mrs Fields office. "We were all rooting for you, Travis" said one music instructor. Well, to Mr Matthis, later that day, He told me I made a little mistake playing, "The Moorish Dance". I performed it all WRONG. That made me feel deeply Bad. Still, I wasn't part of the Music Program. Not at all.

All that whole month of January, I was so much impulsive. I wasn't getting any sleep. Mrs Field and Lester saw all my symptoms. Even at the radio station I was working at. Few students left me alone and they were cruel. I was Pure Manic.

One Night in last weekend of January, Saturday evening, it was wet and rainy. I went to Kentucky Fried Chicken. I brought a chicken snack and I went to Lester's place. He had all his Friends, Felicia and his Kids. Lester knew I was "Hyper as Hell". The night before, I Was all out, I got drunked and crashed at his apartment on his couch in the den. I slept for "3 hours" Lester told me. I wasn't getting any Rest. Again, still wasted and drunk. Felicia said, "Travis is depressed".

Now, on this Saturday night, I was a Lester's place and I got something to eat at KFC. As we were watching TV. Lester spoke out loudly, "No thanks, Trav!" as I was eating. I didn't understand what he was talking about. He was with his boys. Now, Skyline was a wild neighborhood. And whenever, Lester shared some stories about himself. He was talking to me about life as I mentioned earlier. I stayed that whole Night. Listening to Hip-Hop. As his friends left. Now, His friends were very "Tough Guys". They were nothing to play with. Lester too. So, we went out in Cold Dark night and he was talking to and another guy. As we went back inside his place. Then all of a sudden, Lester attacked me not physically but Verbally. Accusing me of being selfish when I bought my meal and not sharing. He lectured me. "You got problems Kid! You need to some help. I can't help you. You come here with your Chicken. Having your napkin spreaded out and your chicken and eating without asking anybody. We share around here!!" He had me in fear and I thought for sure he was going attack me or pull out his gun and shoot me. During that time, I barely knew him, he was always packed. He continued. "My kids get scared around you!" I fired back, "I didn't do anything, Man!" Lester wasn't finished at all. "Man, You look like you're gonna get a Gun and shoot everybody". He was making feel Guilty and be aware of myself. Pointing out my mistakes and my problems. Then one of his Boys protested, "Lester, Leave that man alone. Let that man do whatever he want." Lester corrected him, "This is between me and him! But he continued, "You look at people the wrong the way, somebody is going to shoot you to your head." He knew I was a wreck and about to snap. I was bringing up something about my past in high school. "They were calling me names!" "WHO???, Lester asked. "Some boys from high school??" That's not my problem, All that I'm Saying, Eat before you Come Here!!!"

So, after He lectured me. I left his apartment He said, "Good luck." I was thinking, "Do I really need help?" I was confused. Really. I was hurt by what he was telling me But he was pointing out I need Help. I was wearing down. I didn't know what to do. I was all alone. Darkness befell me. I was confused. I didn't know what to do.

I was troubled deeply. The problems I was having from my childhood to the time I was staying in Winston-Salem, followed me.

Sunday, I went back to Lester's to watch the Super Bowl, The Dallas Cowboys versus The Pittsburgh Steelers. My Cowboys Won. Their revenge from Super Bowl 13 in 1979. Lester was looking at me. He still was looking at me and he was shaking his head. All of his Boys were celebrating. I was Happy and Jubilant too. He knew I was irritable. That night before was still bothering me. So, I never returned to Lester's place. That was it. I had to back off.

But I carried on. I attended my classes. Mrs Fields and Dr Hanson were still my active advisors at the Music Department. Especially, Mrs Fields. The kids at the Radio Station were distancing themselves from me. One absurd lady that I worked with cursed me out because I corrected her about an issue involving Jazz music. And few others too. My Boss, Mr Washington was concerned about me. He knew that I wanted to be a Radio Announcer. He would even discuss to me about my behavior.

FEBRUARY 1996

Mrs Clara Fields, my music instructor, was suggesting that I needed to speak to a counselor. At least, she was someone I could lean on. After my almost physical confrontation with that creep in my Piano Minor I class. The new audition didn't mean Shit to me. To a few members of that Music Faculty, I was a Balled up piece of notebook paper thrown in a trash bucket.

Mr Williams warned me. Indeed. Yet, it wasn't over for me.

During the time I was at Winston-Salem, I attended the St Benedict the MOOR Catholic Church. A small church that assists the needs to the African-American and the Spanish-American Catholic communities. I befriended one Lady who was from Fayetteville and she attended St Ann Catholic Church!! A small world. Of course. She knew some of the people who attended there. Whenever she saw me I was her "Homey from Fayetteville".

Wednesday, February 14th. Valentine's Day arrived, that morning after my Music Theory II class, I came by Mrs Fields and I asked her if she could be my Valentine. She greatly accepted. She was being very helpful as always. She was my Deep inspiration. She gave me a little card. I felt a little better. But inside, I was bitterly boiling.

That weekend, I wasn't getting any rest or sleep at all earlier from that month. Days was going on and on. I was wide open. I was feeling really disturbed. I'll try to explain the ordeal I endure but it's very difficult.

I didn't go anywhere that weekend. I tossed and turned in my Bed. My roommate Oscar didn't even know what I was going through. That Sunday morning, February 18th, I woke up. My dark room had a little sunlight. I went to get a shower and shave. I returned to my room. My second floor Dorm was quiet. I didn't even hear anything. Complete Silence. There were no parties or anything. Just complete silence. I decided to attend Church. I went to the closet. I put on my dark green shirt, my dark beige dress khakis, my black socks and my black Stacy Adams-like shoes. I walked out of my room with my keys and got into my Blue Turquoise 1992 GEO-METRO XFI. And I drove to St Benedict the Moor Catholic Church. I was just going to church hopefully to make me feel better. I arrived. I was there. The weather was cool spring-like with Sunny-Blue Skies. I was at the Church. Lent was about to begin. As the Mass service started, I was just quiet and reserved. I was feeling very shooked up. At the end of Mass. I hardly spoke to anyone except the nice Lady from Fayetteville, (who attended St Ann Church). I left. I was walking slow. I wasn't feeling Right. As I was returning to the campus on MLK Jr Drive, I saw a car with some of the Girls from school and I saw the one Girl who cruelly rejected me a few weeks before. THAT TRIGGERED IT!!! I didn't get over that because it was recent. Tensions within me was growing. I came back to school. I got out of my Car. I was walking slowly to my dorm. I got to my room. My roommate was asleep. I took off my Shoes and I tried to take a nap. I adjusted the curtains of my room. I desperately tried to sleep. I laid on my bed.

The Past. The Past. St Ann School. Hillcrest Junior High. Terry Sanford High. The California Trip. REJECTION. McDonald's. EVERYTHING!! ANYTHING!! EVERYTHING!! WHEN IS THIS GOING END??!! I was feeling being beaten by everyone I dealt with. I was feeling Bitten inside. Feeling Bitten. The Stigma. The persecution. The Prejudice. CRAZY. STALKER. TED BUNDY. WACKO. CRAZY MF. I couldn't Rest or Sleep. My EXTREME Anger was taking over me. I was shaking. I felt I was Being Flogged by Everyone. People. Everyone. The Whip was cracking. I was tied to a post. I couldn't fight back. I got quickly from my bed. I got on the Phone and Called Mrs Fields. Thank God. She answered. My voice was Feeling Heavy. "Mrs Fields, I don't Feel right", I said pleafully. "I don't feel right". I was sounding like a whimpering puppy being beaten. BEATEN!. "I don't Feel right". Mrs Fields asked me immediately, "Do you feel suicidal?" "No" "I just... don't feel.. right.." I was shaking. I was holding my phone tightly. I closed my eyes. I couldn't bother Mrs Fields anymore because she had one of her two sons to deal with. So, I told her that I will go to this Charter Behavioral Health as I looked in the phone book. "Call me back and let me know what's going on." I hung my phone. There was a slight change of Clothes for me. So, this was it. I AM THE GIFT. I was determined to Get Help. I AM THE GIFT. I left in my car. I was keeping myself up. I just didn't feel right. I AM THE GIFT.

It was a 10-15 minute drive. As I was listening to Jimi Hendrix on my pull out radio-cassette player. ELECTRIC LADYLAND album. The Sun was out as the skies was still blue that afternoon. I arrive at the Charter Behavioral Health System of Winston-Salem. It was a fairly big building. I walked in the lobby and It was quiet. I went to the reception desk. I asked to check-in. The receptionist gave me a form to fill out with a clip board attached to it. And I filled out the form as much as I could when I sat in the nice comfortable couch. I gave the receptionist my completed form. I waited for a few minutes. Then, a stout lady walked towards me. She had light brown hair and she wore glasses. She looked very concerned. She sat down on the couch. Her name was Lauren Hurst. She looked at me. Introduced herself. She gently and kindly asked, "What's the matter, Travis?" "Why are you Angry?" She could see that I was shaking. I answered softly, "I feel like I want to hurt someone. I want to get a baseball bat and bash someone's head with it." "Why do you want to hurt someone?" So, I shared with her some issues from my past. She suggested that I should check-in and they would help me and get my treatment started. But it proved to be Expensive and I had no medical insurance. Then she suggested that I should go to Forsyth Stokes Mental Health. "They're not expensive and they can help you so you don't have to be with those cruel people." Then Lauren asked me very seriously, "You're not going to hurt anyone? " No, I won't. I will go back to my dorm." "You're sure?" Lauren asked me. "Yes,

I'm not going to hurt anyone" I assured her. She wrote her business card the facility and the number of Forsyth Stokes Mental Health and gave it to me. So, I drove back to my dorm and I stayed there. I never left my room. I called Back Mrs Fields later that evening and I asked her about the location of this Forsyth Stokes Mental Health. She answered me and gave me the address and she gave me the directions to the Clinic. "When you leave the campus. You make a right on Martin Luther King Jr Drive. You keep going straight on down. Over the bridge. You'll pass the Seafood Market. You'll see a McDonald's on your left. You'll see the Big Building Behind it. That's the Forsyth Stokes Mental Health." Let me know what happens." She sounded very concerned. I also told her that I won't be attending Classes tomorrow. So that's what I did.

Monday. February 19, 1996. It was much colder that day. Blue Skies and Sunny. But this was the most important day for me. A most crucial day in my life. I got up. Put on my clothes. Drove to the Forsyth Stokes Mental Health Center. It didn't take me long to reach the institution.

I was there. I was there. A building with a few stories. It was still chilly when I got out my car and slowly walked inside the building.

I walked inside and it didn't take me long find the receptionist and she handed me the clip board with the form and I did the same thing. I filled it out. And when they called me in. I sat on a nice couch. A few people, they were probably Social Workers or Therapists. I knew there was a Psychiatrist. A nice woman who had a thick accent I guess she was from the Caribbean or African. So, I sat there on the couch. They had their notepads and pens looking and studying at this poor young individual. Me. I was so nervous and my eyes were shifting. Then came the questions, "What's the matter, Travis? You wrote you're going to hurt someone." I mumbled and I could barely speak, "I feel like I'm in high school again". They wrote and jotted down notes. I stood still and shaking at the same time. I was winding down. I needed help. They could see my condition. I wanted to sacrifice myself. Then the female psychiatrist looked at me with concern and she said simply, "You need to be on Lithium."

So, I agreed to be a patient. I went another office and sat down. A very nice lady, another receptionist looked at me with sympathy. I had to fill a lot of paperwork to officially confirm myself a patient at the Forsyth Stokes Mental Health Center. "It's going to be alright." We're going help you," She assured me kindly. After that I went to the nursing room. And a male nurse, a "brother", already had my information. "Wassup Travis? I'm going to need a Blood sample and a Urine sample." He gave me a cup in a plastic wrap. "I'm going to need your urine. Keep it in a fridge for 2 days. And when you come back, then I get your blood sample. Okay?" I was still looking troubled. I nodded and followed the nurse's instructions on what I had to do.

I walked out of the building. I felt ashamed. I was feeling the cold air as I walked to my car in the parking lot. I had my head down. Then those thoughts was coming to my head. "He finally realized he's CRAZY after all!!" I was feeling awful, sad and miserable. Feeling punched from the Past. But I had to look at the Bright side....I was getting Help. The way I was feeling had to suppress. I had repeated doubts. Is this what I needed? Was this the right decision for me to make?

I returned to the campus. Yes, I did. I went to the Fine Arts Building and spoke with Mrs Clara Fields in her office. She nodded as she was preparing herself a Cup of coffee. She agreed that it was the right decision for me to make. But she was still there for me as well as Dr Hanson.

As I walked out of the Fine Arts building, I had to keep my head up. The cold morning. I was getting help. I was still crossing those terrible desert sands, the raging storms and robber bands. The Star will appear. I am the GIFT. Finally, An air breeze of Silent Peace gently fell upon me.

TO BE CONTINUED.......

CPSIA information can be obtained
at www.ICGtesting.com
Printed in the USA
JSHW032155201222
35250JS00001B/21